Nineveh:
a
Parody
of the
Present

Biblical Clues
to the Rise and Fall
of America

Mobile, Alabama

Nineveh: A Parody of the Present
by Victor Schlatter
Copyright ©2009 Victor Schlatter

All rights reserved. This book is protected under the copyright laws of the United States of America. This book may not be copied or reprinted for commercial gain or profit. Unless otherwise identified, Scripture quotations are taken from *THE HOLY BIBLE: New International Version* ©1978 by the New York International Bible Society, used by permission of Zondervan Bible Publishers. Scriptures marked MSG are taken from *THE MESSAGE*. Copyright © by Eugene H. Peterson 1993, 1994, 1995, 1996, 2000, 2002. Used by permission of NavPress Publishing Group. All rights reserved.

ISBN 978-1-58169-325-6
For Worldwide Distribution
Printed in the U.S.A.

Evergreen Press
P.O. Box 191540 • Mobile, AL 36619
800-367-8203
www.evergreenpress.com

TABLE OF CONTENTS

Dedicated to the King of Zion
Psalm 2:1-6

Why do the nations conspire,
and the peoples plot in vain?

The kings of the earth
take their stand
and the rulers gather together
against the Lord
and against his Anointed One.

"Let us break their chains"
they say,
"and throw off their fetters."

The One enthroned in heaven
laughs; the Lord scoffs at them.

Then he rebukes them in his anger
and terrifies them in his wrath,
saying, "I have installed my
King on Zion
my holy hill."

FOREWORD

This book is certainly not about challenging the political posturing of the nations amongst whom we dwell in these traumatic times. In fact, I pray that you will find these pages far different than the media sensationalism on which we are force-fed daily, including the mutually discredited ideologies or innuendoes of scarcely veiled hatred and distrust.

I daily read an immense amount of articles, opinions, reports, and news analyses these days, and they virtually all quite naively miss the glaring point on one extraordinary consideration: GOD!

So much speculation is made and so much advice is given on what human governments ought or ought not to do to reverse the flow of divine destiny. In spite of political posturing and promises, can the human leopard change his spots? We all get a tsunami of emails of what *they*—whoever *they* happens to be—should be doing to solve the global crises. But can they? Will they? I suggest a similar success rate with those hoax email windfalls of fortune that lure the fool to his downfall. No less ludicrous, be it prince or pauper, is the citizen who allows the Almighty to mindlessly slip out of the equation of human destiny under any government.

The Ancient of Days, who was, who is, and who will be, can be counted on to remain in charge for yet a few eons more! Unfortunately a perverse and godless media along with the self-centered kings of the earth avoid any hint of His involvement like the plague! He's an unworthy gate crasher if He exists at all.

Our research in these pages points to biblical clues on the Rise and Fall of America. But it's hardly about a sole superpower nearing her end of days. We will compare superpowers from the beginning. What was yesterday is yet a part of today, and will still be here tomorrow. The Play Dough of eternity is not about to change. The Good Book assures us it won't. Nineveh, Babylon, Greece, Rome, yesterday's Europe, and today's America are ever with us, along with "wars and rumours of war," but ultimately a New Jerusalem!

So unless the Bible is all wrong and the Hellenistic humanists are indeed correct—but they're not doing all that well with their gods of gold at the moment!—the King of the Universe is not about to jettison His designer galaxy to the junkyard of history just yet!

Hopefully we'll all learn something to celebrate tomorrow's dawn.

INTRODUCTION

Back in September 2008—which just happened to be my 22nd visit to Jerusalem—I found myself encountering a wide-eyed 2AM jet lag which prompted me to cancel the normal pursuit of a night's rest. Plan B soon beckoned me to slip silently downstairs into a comfy B & B Guest House lounge room and catch up instead on a bit of review of the Hebrew prophets.

I reckoned I'd get into a couple of my favorite books like a few of the opening and closing chapters of Job, as well as a possible run through Jonah once more. Jonah is one of the books we had studied a decade earlier when my wife and I were learning to read biblical Hebrew. The runaway prophet had always been a winner with me long before pursuing it in Hebrew. And Jonah was the shorter of the two options, so I started on him first.

Now in the very first verse of the very first chapter, this name Nineveh comes up which anyone who knows about Jonah knows Nineveh as well. It's a whale of a story! (OK, so it wasn't actually a whale, but it was a "big fish.")

But it so happened that as I'm just getting started, I see this cross-reference note on Nineveh that directs me over to the Prophet Nahum—a tiny prophetic message of a mere three chapters. That's even shorter than Jonah! So Jonah gets put on hold, and Nahum wins pole position! I hadn't read Nahum for quite a while. But then Abba began to open my eyes even wider than my 2 AM jet lag.

The four chapters of Jonah were about Nineveh's redemption. But the three chapters of Nahum were about her ultimate and untimely reversal—judgment by the King of the Universe! Moreover, the Prophet Nahum reflected some uncomfortable parallels of a Hellenistic, hedonistic and humanistic Western world of the 21st century!

Then Abba nudged me and said, "Look, I want you to write

your next book." But I began to dig my heels in a bit with: "That's going to be a lot more work for this season of my life, and my friends have been telling me to slow down a tad! Anyway, this B & B place is not my normal mode of abode. And I don't want to entertain any pretentious promptings that might be pandering around this uncharted parlor."

And then I kind of looked up and said, "Is that really You that's telling me these things?"

I wanted to make sure. So I gave Him a proposal that night and put out three fleeces. If you don't know what that means, check it out in Chapter 6 in the Book of Judges. Gideon made a couple of unconventional lab tests with a sheepskin to see if it was really God that was talking or maybe some other uninvited and otherwise extraneous entity?

So I decided to ask Abba for three things:

1. "If this is really Your idea, there's going to have to be enough funds to carry it out." This was sort of a non-starter. We mortals may not always have the immediate means to maneuver, but the Almighty "owns the cattle on a thousand hills," and if He gets an idea, funding is not an issue!

2. "Next, provide us a place in Israel to hide away from society for a few months until I can get the manuscript prepared." This one was a bit harder. I guess I wouldn't have to, but I've written all my books in Israel. The celestial communication there seems to be a bit clearer. If you don't understand this, maybe you've never been to Israel. True, their political echelon doesn't actually seem to be the one who routinely maintains a hotline with the Dove from Above, but not a few others—including a variety of visitors—do notice a sense of nearness that is not normal to the more mundane places they have travelled. So that was request No. 2 for fleece No. 2.

3. "And if Kenyan-rooted, Wahabbist-schooled, Junior Senator-

out-of-nowhere, Barack Hussein Obama, gets elected President of the United States on November the 4th, I'm listening, Lord! I'll write what You tell me!"

Those were the three fleeces. But then an unscheduled fleece No. 4 surfaced as soon as I returned back home to Australia at the end of October 2008. Before I ever left home five months earlier in May, my doctor had this thing about my ever-lengthening years, an occasional pain or two in the wrong place, cardiac tests, and the like. He kept bugging me to get a stress test way back then. And so I finally did; unfortunately, I failed it!

But there was no time at that short notice before we left on the Israel circuit for the medical masters to carry out the brutal business of jamming a tube up an artery! (Thinking about this sort of nonsense nearly creates an acute attack of something—for most male members of the species anyway!) But the constraint of time spared me from this untimely treachery in May, so they put it off until I returned back home in October. I hoped my doc would even forget about it! Well, he wouldn't, and he didn't! The Cardiac Clinic ironically scheduled the angiogram for that very same week as those Obama elections. How fleecy can you get?

And sure enough, the controversial candidate did win the election! Plus it was quite clear that there would be funds enough for travel. And even though we had no offer of a house in Israel, a tempting little hide-away substitute became available that very same week in the rolling Tablelands, a pleasant plateau just above and beyond our home in Cairns.

And wouldn't you know, that cruelly crafted but none the less crucial cardiac test showed my little pink pump to be in perfect condition. Hallelujah!

Nothing like keeping all your fleeces in one basket! "I think I got the message, Abba. I'll start writing immediately!"

The only hitch might have been that those pleasant Tablelands are not exactly Jerusalem, but the real thing abruptly did fall into place with precision fulfillment. Abba came through with an obviously preplanned 8-10 week setting on a hilltop overlooking the Sea of Galilee just above Tiberius.

So, taking off from Jonah and Nahum combined, we're now going to have a look at *Nineveh: A Parody of the Present* with even deeper insight meandering through "Biblical Clues on the Rise and Fall of America." Hopefully we'll pick up on some trails that have been little trodden, if at all. Come with me.

Not sure how many of you know that Nineveh's modern name is Mosul in Iraq, situated about 400km northwest of Baghdad. Mosul even made notorious headlines this last week when some of the local lads had been executing Christians gangland style. Perhaps not all that much has permanently changed in Nineveh since Nimrod, infamous hunter and blood letter, who featured in her first foundation stones. But that's hardly the real shadow that the parody which is Nineveh casts across the globe in our day. This new book should give us even much, much more to ponder.

We'll begin by probing what the Bible refers to as *the nations*, proceeding to a peek at the biblical superpowers of bygone days, following their rise, demise, and life-span from Nineveh to now. But throughout the journey, never dare we ever overlook Solomon's immortal watchword of inescapable wisdom: *"There's nothing new under the sun."*

Victor Schlatter
Upper Tiberius, Israel

CHAPTER 1

Just Who Are *The Nations?*

On September 11, 2001 nineteen Wahabbists—fourteen of them from problematic Prince Ishmael's ancient Arabian deserts—clipped off the Twin Towers of the World Trade Center. Unbelievably seven years and 54 days later, a most unlikely one-time grade school student in that same Jakarta-based Wahabbist educational system, succeeded in securing the presidency of that troubled, once proud nation, confounding many of its Christians. But he did it far more delicately with a boisterous home-grown ballot box instead of a pair of roaring 747s.

For better or worse, November 4, 2008 exploded the 232-year myth—at least held by some—that theologically transferred Genesis over to the Gentiles, genetically modified Deuteronomy into democracy, and postulated that the USA had long since divinely replaced Israel as God's Chosen People. Her claims as a favored light among the nations, her favored superpower status among the starry host complete with godly pledges of faith, faithfulness, and trust in the God of heaven, lay neatly folded at the feet of a once-upon-a-time Islamic rooted Kenyan Luo tribesman. It was a proud nation that had naively claimed a tad of control—if not an outright corner on the market—of the Creator of the universe for some 232 years.

Shall I say that again? The election of November 2008 should have abruptly awakened America to the fact that the Western oriented Church had *not* replaced Israel after all. Moreover, it should

1

also be abundantly evident in this latter-day wakeup call that the Church was never given the mandate to control God. And politically, it's a whole new ball game with Islam in the race for global supremacy! Sadly those saints who were the most sure of their doctrinally modified divinity still slumber on!

No unchallenged civilization—no democracy—has lasted much more than two centuries. And no nation, no matter how saintly, spiritual, God-fearing, and anointed gets much longer than that to presume spiritual priority as the holy ones of heaven. Abba picks the kings and queens as well as the pawns of His international chess board—not Caesar, not Constantine, not King George VI nor even George Washington the 1st or GW the 2nd. Only Abba!

Please, my friend, this is neither a tirade of politics nor an undermining attack of the new President of the United States of America. I pray for him; I wish him well. But bizarre beginnings are bizarre beginnings, strange facts are strange facts, and an unknown future is an unknown future, which to Bible believers unquestionably belongs to the God of *the nations*.[1]

The Table of Nations

And who might *the nations* be? Saudi Arabia is one of them; Egypt is yet another. And America is yet one more. And there is much, much more explanation to come.

The Holy Writ from the meanderings of Moses to the miracles of the Messiah uses the term *the nations* some 200 times depending on how often the translators chose to just use the plural pronoun "they" instead. Anyway, just who are these people? Like anything else, it depends a tad on the terms of reference of your definition, so let's probe the possibilities.

First of all, if we're only looking for a list, that's easy enough. In Genesis 10, we'll find them all right there in black and white. The chapter heading—coined by the translator in most English translations—is: "The Table of Nations."

This might be a good place to note, however, that those headings suggested by the translators may be a bit helpful, but not exactly as sanctified as the inspired messages that follow on after them. We regard those ancient writers as divinely inspired, whereas, we translators who only manufacture those literary "milemarkers" (aka headings) between the various biblical concepts could be a bit more prone to error. So just a word to the wise: Latter-day translators (as early as 18th century scholars and even earlier) can and should be quite good, but even then they have been known to miss the mark on occasion. Some have been found to steer long-misunderstood passages into garden-path diversions with their headings. So be careful!

Having said that, "The Table of Nations" title seems quite legitimate, so let's get on with that one. Chapter 10 lists the offspring of the three sons of Noah—Shem, Ham, and Japheth—their sons, and in some cases several of their grandsons and even beyond. These were the proud papas of whom the Designer of the Universe came to regard as *the nations.*

Simple enough! That's where we all came from. If you're an anthropologist, you can get into Wikipedia and head out (occasionally undetected) from there! In fact, we personally knew anthropologists from Papua New Guinea who made up their own stuff. If you're crafty, you can concoct a thesis and sell it to your department head for thousands! I'm not kidding! Who can prove this research anyway unless you happen to have been a Bible translator and lived closely among some of these indigenous folks for a few decades and discover what little those so-called scientific studies by some of the anthropologists really amount to! Unfortunately many of the media documentaries blatantly come up with similar fiction to feed the far-removed stranger who unwittingly also pays in quite good coin!

Anyway some—I'm hardly saying all—anthropologists and media documentaries will also give us their take about *the nations,* but that's another genus of garden path, so let's waste no more time on these dubious diversions. We must soon move on to places like Nineveh and Babylon where the globe has shrunk so significantly that even folks we know who have been there can clarify a few of the renegade reports.

Abraham's Family Is Not
To Be Counted as one of *The Nations*

Yet another way of definition is what *the nations* are not. Now it is pretty clear from the Good Book, that if you are from the off-spring of Abraham, Isaac, and Jacob you are *not* included as one of *the nations*.

How can that be? Well God Himself told them that they weren't to be counted as one of *the nations*.[2] The pagan prophet, Balaam, even made this a point in his unconventional prophecy to the King of Moab, when instead of cursing Israel as the obsessed king had demanded, he said:

From the rocky peaks I see them; From the heights I view them; I see a people who live apart, and do not consider themselves one of the nations.[3]

How this all started was that the Almighty took Abraham out-side on a beautifully clear night, had him check out those mega-millions of stars, and made him a promise that this celestial panorama was a symbol of his future family-to-be. The essence was that this display of destiny showed the difference between the basic family of Abraham and all the rest.

Of special significance, however, was that some of those others were actually able to be drawn from out of *the nations* to be added to and included with those original people of promise as we shall shortly see. But for now, if we think of the offspring of Abraham as symbolized by all those stars, then to really secure the memorable metaphor, *the nations* might well be represented by the intervening darkness that was punctuated by the spectacular. Not a bad analogy, perhaps!

So before we go further, I wrote all about the relevant activities and attributes of Abraham in my previous book, *Where is the Body?*, so let's not repeat these redundancies here. If you're not familiar with it, I suggest you check out some fine tuning into parallel insights on what we are searching out here.[4]

The Creator's Curious Treasure

But now let's have a look at another unique separation of the men from the boys (or should we say the sharks from the sardines). It's in Exodus 19:4-6a and took place at the foot of the awesome ascendancy of Sinai, the Mount of God:

> *You yourselves have seen what I did to Egypt, and how I carried you on eagles' wings and brought you to myself. Now if you obey me fully and keep my covenant, then out of all nations you will **be my treasured possession**. Although the whole earth is mine, you will be for me a kingdom of priests and a holy nation* (emphasis added).

God's chosen pet pansies? Ask any Jew about their "chosen" primrose path. *"If you obey me fully and keep my covenant..."* is more like a selection of an elite unit of Special Forever Forces. The training is tough! The nations will hate you. Their media will manufacture misinformation. You will become the butt of their jibes.

One of their own prophesied that *"all men (of the nations) will hate you because of me."*[5] They will be jealous of your Nobel prizes in science and medicine, your brilliance in banking or your expertise in gaining wealth. Unfortunately these attributes neither save you nor get you the kind of friends you need. But they are valuable tools in life's survival, and they are real!

Nevertheless, the deck of *the nations* is stacked against you. (Did you ever visit a Holocaust Memorial?) Being a "treasured possession" of the One who has always had not a few problems with all the other nations is a bit uphill. Just ask Moses!

An Open Door for Outsiders—An Exit for the Unimpressed

But lest you make too many sterile assumptions about a selection to be separate from *the nations*, let's note that the genetics of this thing is neither cast in concrete nor chiseled in stone (actually the covenant was!). You can get in or out at will. That's why a lot of today's secular Jews (should I say leftist?) are neither impressed with their promises nor their options! But who knows? With the right kind of friends and the right set of circumstances, things could get significantly brighter. Abba's not as inept as some of them might think!

> *The path of the righteous is like the first gleam of dawn,*
> *shining ever brighter till the full light of day.*[6]

But on the other side of the coin, those across time who have seen the Light of the Covenant begin perhaps with Jethro, Moses' father-in-law; we then proceed to Caleb the Kenizzite;[7] then Rahab the Inn Keeper;[8] Ruth the Moabitess; and Bathsheba the widow. Then there was another widow of Zarephath;[9] the Roman centurion of Matthew 9:5; the Canaanite woman of Matthew 15:21; the Samaritan woman of John 4; and there was Cornelius, another Roman officer of Acts 10. Timothy and Titus were both of mixed Greek heritage—the list of non-Hebraic genetics is endless across Scripture!

Yet even more massive are the grafted-in olive branches of Romans 11, which is a front and center stage feature of the one and only *chosen* nation versus a broad generalization of *the nations*.[10]

The bottom line is that there is a revolving door within the chosen nation of promise to let the disenchanted out and the distinctly elect in. First Peter 2:4-12 summarizes precisely the function of Zion's promised Messiah. Have a look at it in its entirety. But to make sure you don't miss the geographic location of this favored nation, I want to call your special attention to verse 6:

> *For in Scripture it says: "See, I lay a stone in **Zion**, a chosen and precious cornerstone, and the one who trusts in him will never be put to shame"* (emphasis added).

Moreover, pointing to the ethnic structure of a less than politically postured nation, initially chosen at the foot of Mount Sinai but expanded significantly at the foot of Mount Calvary (aka Mount Moriah), we encounter *the one and only chosen nation* as presented from the same text in Peter's epistle, verses 9 and 10:

> *But you are a chosen people, a royal priesthood, a holy nation, a people belonging to God, that you may declare the praises of him who called you out of darkness into his wonderful light. Once you were not a people, but now you are the people of God; once you had not received mercy, but now you have received mercy.*

Thus we are presented with a predominantly Hebraic oriented, but also multi-ethnic people of God while *the nations* per se are peeking in through the international cracks.

It should therefore come as no surprise to *the nations*—who from Genesis to Revelation are *always* regarded as political outsiders to a Kingdom of Principles—that neither China (the King of Creation made a lot of them!) nor Russia, not the British nor the Irish, the French, the Germans, or even the Americans are suggested in Scripture as the "apple of His eye"!

Now not too many seasoned scholars should get it confused what nation the Almighty is referring to in Deuteronomy 32:7-10, or whose chosen family is the apple of His eye.

> *Remember the days of old; consider the generations long past. Ask your father and he will tell you, your elders, and they will explain to you. When the Most High gave the nations their inheritance, when he divided all mankind, he set up boundaries*

*for the peoples according to the number of the sons of Israel. For the Lord's portion is his people, Jacob his allotted inheritance. In a desert land he found him, in a barren and howling waste. He shielded him and cared for him; he guarded him as the **apple of his eye**...* (emphasis added).

Nor should they blindly confuse the identity of "the apple of His eye" whom Zechariah was urging to escape from Babylon and her gods in Zechariah 2:7-8

*Come, O Zion! Escape, you who live in the Daughter of Babylon!' For this is what the Lord Almighty says: "After he has honored me and has sent me against the nations that have plundered you—For whoever touches you touches the **apple of his eye**"* (emphasis added).

Indeed there were those Hebrews (aka Jews in this context) who refused their roles and abdicated their responsibilities from the days of Moses on through Yeshua,[11] who himself actually reinforced Moses' principles from beginning to end. But those dropouts hardly served to take Abba's eye off His chosen channel to rescue His sons of redemption, adopted or otherwise.

Replacing Replacement Theology With the Real Thing

But there were still others of Gentile vintage, who have been ambitious to capture their own crowns via a back door of theological substitutions and nationalistic pride. These would turn their nation(s) of personal preference into anti-Semitic applesauce to chalk up a few points of their own self-styled spiritual status "outside the camp."

I stumbled across a website recently where one misguided blogger was berating those of us who have ultimately recognized that God's plan from the beginning was to choose—and use—one family out of *the nations* to serve as a pilot project—complete with

Pilot—for global redemption from *both* inside and outside of the Family of Promise.

Since not a few Bible believers are catching the vision these days to both prayerfully and prophetically watch for the final act to unfold, it undoubtedly triggered our website wizard to fire back a few volleys of his own. It must have disturbed him that far too much focus of the saints has been shifting to a secular Israel gone bonkers! Obviously he had missed a few biblical facets somewhere along the way, but never mind his oversight. We all make mistakes!

Presumptuously, he proffered the absurd question that if all nations were destroyed but America or Israel, which of those two nations would your pastor advise his faithful flock would be the obvious divine choice to be left standing?

His hoped-for response would have been anything but a secular, renegade Israel—that improbable 1948 implant of violence into the Middle East! To be sure, if "Christian" America were the choice of the only nation left standing, they would soon flood the sons of Ishmael with so many missionaries that even the Saudis would likely drown in a sea of salvation. And that doesn't even mention the bountiful benefits to the rest of the globe!

Unfortunately, this hardly clarifies why this phenomenon of faith hasn't happened up to now, nor why persecution of true believers is by contrast on the rise in America—just as it is everywhere else in the world. But that might well blunt his point. Nor would it seem to occur to him that the sons of Ishmael are no more impressed with American methodology than many of the sons of Jacob happen to be at this point of time.

Now this is so dumb that it's hardly worth the mention, but actually it turns out to be of value. Some folks are so far out of the Scriptures and into the secular merchandising methods of the mall, that their copyrighted system of salvation has long superseded the significance of intimacy with the Savior Himself. And this doesn't even take into account Abba's[12] own personal planning as the curtain falls on the end of days![13]

Standing back a bit to see what really happened, the opening breath of the Holy Book in Genesis 1:1 declares, *"In the beginning God..."* The final benediction of Revelation 22:21 in the NIV is: *"The grace of the Lord Jesus be with God's people..."* The King James version and some earlier translations only say, *"...with you **all**."* Fair enough, that's an accurate rendition, but the NIV and several others clarify who "all" would include. It is both helpful and even legitimate to also translate the implicit information in the text. This text means without question, "all God's people." The message of the Eternal One begins with "God," and finalizes with "God's People." From Alpha to Omega, He created an eternal family to be His very own friends—or from Mount Sinai dialog, should we say: *"His treasured possession."*

This hardly minimizes that midway He prepared the Chosen One from the very root of the People of Promise[14] for the redemption of the faithful. But *how* He did it was hardly a theological end in itself to be venerated as God's cleverness, but rather the catalyst of God's Son to the ultimate end that a Family of Fellowship, "a chosen people, a holy nation" were reborn.

In the beginning *God*—and in the end *God,* along with the rest of *His Family,* that obviously included His first born Son!

Unfortunately there are those who out of bias, blindness, or nationalistic ambition, tend to drop the ball at the most crucial time. Ironically, it all reflects back to Israel's ancient King Saul, who as an exact mirror-image opposite to the Son of Man, shed his life blood on the wrong mountain—Mt. Gilboa. Because of personal ambition, King Saul got it wrong! Thus, David's lament for his fallen leader: *"How the mighty have fallen."*[15]

May we have learned the lesson that from Genesis through Revelation, *the nations* are but political entities that, in the idolatrous fashion of ancient Israel, are *never* to be substituted for the real thing: *The Apple of His eye.*

We will learn in the following chapters that from Nineveh to Nebraska, true believers are forever welcome to come out from under their nationalistic icons to a New Jerusalem that contains no ethnic ascendancies, but rather an eternal association with the one and only sovereign power—the King of the Jews.

May we not, like King Saul, fall short on the wrong mountain—a bit too far from Jerusalem!

1 See Deuteronomy 29:29 that presents us with the lion's share of theological posers!
2 See Exodus 33:16 and 1 Sam 8:5 and 20.
3 Numbers 23:9.
4 Victor Schlatter, *Where Is the Body?* (Shippensburg, PA: Destiny Image Publishers, 1999), Chapter 1, "A Man Called Abraham."
5 See Mark 13:13 and John 15:20-21
6 Proverbs 4:18
7 Joshua 14:6; 1 Chronicles 4:13-15.
8 Joshua 2; Matthew 1:5; Hebrews 11:31
9 1 Kings 17:7-24
10 Review Romans 11:11-24 for comprehensive cover of the significance of the Olive Tree symbolism.
11 *Yeshua* is the Hebraic rendition of Jesus which I use throughout this volume.
12 The reader may have noticed that I like to call him *Abba*
13 Compare with Matthew 24:36
14 See Isaiah 11:1, 10; Romans 15:12; Revelation 5:5; 22:16
15 2 Samuel 1:19

CHAPTER 2

If It's Not Russia, Just Who Is Prince Gog?

Okay. So now we have some solid insight from the Good Book on the Creator's definition of—or should we say design of—*the nations*.

Secular America happens to be one of them and so is secular Russia, but an Abba-oriented Israel is *not*. Rather Israel is primarily an eternal Pilot Project to provide what all *the nations*—along with the spiritual dimension of Israel—could and should be. Mentioning Israel's spiritual dimension is of course significant. Note that we said: *Abba*-oriented Israel, not *Ahab*-oriented Israel. That spells quite a difference!

Now our title notes Nineveh and also points to America, but it doesn't mention word one about this has-been Communist superpower of yesteryear. So how are we going to let the Russian Bear of once-upon-a-time political pomp nuzzle her way to the front of my book? Well it's because there's a lot of prophetic hype out about this one-time giant of the Gulag that may not be totally true. Some of it is, of course, but let's not be looking at the wrong mountain should the Bear happen to go over it!

Russia and Armageddon

Let's have a look into at least one of the suppositions associated with this slightly demoted superpower of latter days—Russia.

In the 38th and 39th chapters of the writings of the prophet Ezekiel there are some interesting predictions associated with a name that almost everyone knows—Armageddon! But that's hardly to say that the multitudes have much of a clear idea of what Armageddon is all about. They just know the name and sense it's bad news! So let's go biblical.

Interestingly enough, Ezekiel doesn't even mention Armageddon in his writings, but it is clear from the finale of the battle described in Revelation 9:16, plus a few other scattered references to a place called Megiddo located in the Jezreel Valley,[1] that this is the precise site of the horrific conflict he is telling us about in chapters 38 and 39.

Yet in spite of the masses who *have* heard of the horror predictions of Armageddon, only a limited number from the Bible-oriented few, have also heard of the involvement of a Prince Gog at the center of the scene. But of all those who *have* heard of this Gog fellow, most perhaps presume that his title is a cryptic clue representing superpower Russia. In fact we have heard this interpretation to be the "God-given" gospel for generations from the most brilliant of Bible buffs.

However, I say this might be an ideal time to slightly apply the brakes. Let's have a look at two key Scriptures from prophet Ezekiel. Ezekiel 38:1-6 says this:

> *The word of the LORD came to me: Son of man, set your face against Gog, of the land of Magog, the chief prince of Meshech and Tubal; prophesy against him and say: "This is what the Sovereign LORD says: I am against you, O Gog, chief prince of Meshech and Tubal. I will turn you around, put hooks in your jaws and bring you out with your whole army—your horses, your horsemen fully armed, and a great horde with large and small shields, all of them brandishing their swords. Persia, Cush and Put will be with them, all with shields and helmets, also Gomer with all its troops, and Beth Togarmah from the far north with all its troops—the many nations with you."*

Now this is the prophet's description of the assembly of a massive war maneuver (aka Armageddon) to attack and destroy Israel for forever and a day at the time of the bitter end. And the pros have therefore put a much-mistrusted Russia at the head of this parade of infamy. Maybe? Maybe not!

Let's go to our second text, this time in Ezekiel 39:1-6:

> *Son of man, prophesy against Gog and say: "This is what the Sovereign LORD says: I am against you, O Gog, chief prince of Meshech and Tubal. I will turn you around and drag you along. I will bring you from the far north and send you against the mountains of Israel. Then I will strike your bow from your left hand and make your arrows drop from your right hand. On the mountains of Israel you will fall, you and all your troops and the nations with you. I will give you as food to all kinds of carrion birds and to the wild animals. You will fall in the open field, for I have spoken, declares the Sovereign LORD. I will send fire on Magog and on those who live in safety in the coastlands, and they will know that I am the LORD."*

If not Russia as the prime leader of this less than fruitful foray—then who is it? Or who is *he*?

Gog Who and Prince What's-His-Name Probed in Scripture

The name Gog has thirteen mentions in the Scriptures. The first one is in the genealogy lists found in 1 Chronicles. It happens to be the name of a far-down-the-line offspring of Reuben,[2] eldest son of Jacob. But this particular Gog is so far removed from the Table of the Nations in Genesis 10, that we can forget him fairly fast. Wrong Gog!

And the final biblical mention of the real Gog is in Revelation 20 where—in intimate association with Satan—the somber scenario finalizes in those unfortunate flames.[3]

14

*Satan will be released from his prison and will go out to deceive
the nations in the four corners of the earth—Gog and Magog—
to gather them for battle. In number they are like the sand on
the seashore. They marched across the breadth of the earth and
surrounded the camp of God's people, the city he loves. But fire
came down from heaven and devoured them. And the devil,
who deceived them, was thrown into the lake of burning sulfur,
where the beast and the false prophet had been thrown.*

The context in this verse is not completely clear whether this
foul fellow actually represents a king or a nation, so let's just follow
the clues to our final grasp of the matter.

But all the remaining—11 out of 13—mentions of Prince Gog
are in chapters 38 and 39 of Ezekiel that we first mentioned. Let
us also note that he was identified as a prince—i.e. *not* a nation—in
both of our texts above.

So next, what does it mean to be a prince in biblical understanding? In some 55 give or take references to a *prince* in the sacred pages, a prince is either a wannabe, a gonna-be, or a
gittin'-ready to be.

The only exception to that rule that I can see is the classic reference to the *Prince of Peace* in Isaiah 9:6. But stepping back a bit
to study that one-time usage of *Prince*, it's not really a hard puzzle
to solve. The gonna-be in that imagery is that it's the Peace that is
gonna-be and not the Prince! The I AM *is*! Problem solved!

So with this much insight into the predominate usage of *prince*
in the Scriptures, I'm getting a deep-down feeling that in the end
of it all, Prince Gog is gonna-be a wannabe!

What's Wrong With North?

Now the second question is where does this problem prince
hail from? The *north* absolutely, and our two above texts from
Ezekiel specifically note the *far* north. Now that is what our
Russian backers speculate on, but on the other hand, are there not

a fair few other places from Russia to Rotterdam that are also located to the far north of Israel? (So is Father Christmas, but I doubt that even the worst of theologians will mind too much if we lop him off the short list immediately!)

Out of the some 40 biblical references for the direction north, close to half of them associate the north with devastating attack, demise, or just plain trouble. Sure, Babylon as well as Nineveh are north of Jerusalem, and that is a point well taken. But there are other prophesied attacks that are *not* north of the Promised Land, including other nations prophesied to be in the line of attack. In short, biblically "from the north" is generally bad news. And no one can deny that Gog is less than good tidings. Yet neither does that make him a nation, nor does it line him up with Russia!

Just a bit more probing into the north before we hit some real nuggets of insight. Back in the 70s when we sang Scripture Songs straight out of the King James Bible—and I note my nostalgia for them yet today—there was that chorus of priceless praise from Psalm 48:1-2 in the KJV:

> *Great* [is] *the LORD, and greatly to be praised in the city of our God,* [in] *the mountain of his holiness. Beautiful for situation, the joy of the whole earth,* [is] *mount Zion,* [on] *the sides of the north, the city of the great King.*

Those of us who sang it will never lose its grasp of grandeur to the soul. But there was one troublesome glitch of meaning? What's this, *"…Mount Zion, on the sides of the north"* bit? Except for the NIV, most translations do say "north" but all in varying connection with Mount Zion—and regrettably without any clear meaning of what north might have to do with the Holy Hill. Zion is not north of much of anything well known—except Gaza—and I doubt that's what the sons of Korah [the Psalm was attributed to their authorship] had in heart and mind!

So what did the NIV do with it? At first glance, not much! But wait a minute. Maybe they did, for one clever clue at least:

Great is the Lord, and most worthy of praise, in the city of our God, his holy mountain. It is beautiful in its loftiness, the joy of the whole earth. **Like the utmost heights of Zaphon is Mount Zion, the city of the Great King** (emphasis added).

What or where is Zaphon? *Zaphon* is the Hebrew word for north, but it is also the name of a town on the Golan Heights mentioned in passing in Joshua 13:27 as well as Judges 12:1 in some translations. But the Golan Heights are not all that high and I wouldn't say the NIV made an immense improvement in any link with Zion over what any of the other translators had done. Let me suggest that there's much in old Hebrew that's not the easiest to catch a full significance of what the author had penned. Nevertheless, may we give the NIV a few extra points for their footnote: "Zaphon can refer to **a** *sacred mountain* or the direction of the *north*." Both clues are helpful; the emphasis is mine.

Sacred mountain? Sacred to whom? Abba certainly doesn't mention this heralded hill in the Good Book—that could make it an idolatrous Canaanite shrine!

Digging further into the reference books, we find that variations in the spelling of Zaphon also give us *Saphon*. Most interesting! Mount Saphon is a 1770-meter (5800 feet) highly venerated spur in the Bargylus Mountains just north of the ancient ruins of Ugarit,[4] the high profile capital of the Ugaritic Kingdom that had been situated on what is presently Syria's west coast. The Ugaritic language that is very closely related to Hebrew and Phoenician dialects has been of special interest to Bible translators from that part of the globe outward.

But of even greater interest is the significance of Mount Saphon. It has been determined that Saphon was the Mt. Olympus of Canaanite gods, and the very seat for the religion and cult of their chief deity Baal himself!

So with those findings, might this one-time translator suggest an additional insight that may have been heretofore overlooked?

The sons of Korah may well have been making a comparison of the spiritual majesty of Mount Zion with that long-gone pagan abomination at Ugarit just north of modern Lebanon.

Though Scripture does not suggest that Joshua got anywhere near the northern reaches of Lebanon, calculations do indicate that in taking over from Moses, he would have become the Israelites new leader in approximately 1190 BC. The Book of Joshua details his conquering all the kings of the north that had formed an alliance with the king of Hazor,[5] and further lists these and all the other kings he overthrew, making a grand total of 31 vanquished Canaanite kingdoms listed in Joshua 12.

Ironically anthropology has recently determined that Ugarit's royal palaces, temples, and shrines were destroyed around 1200 BC.[6] On the one hand Joshua never supposedly got that far north, but on the other hand, the matching of the dates looks most interesting!

But what is the bottom line for our present search for the significance of *north* aka Saphon? A Canaanite "Mt. Olympus" styled bastion of Baal would have been well known to a congregation chanting Psalm 48, but long-lost for clear cut meaning by the 20th century era of English Scripture songs. North, indeed!

Thus it does tie in with what we are learning from the Hebrew prophets' point of view that Psalm 48:1-2 and Isaiah 14:14 are no more and no less than the comparison between pagan Mt. Saphon and the incomparably sanctified Mt. Zion. Moreover, the north might *not* be the ideal direction to head for your holidays! But seriously, it more than reinforces what we're going to discover next. Who in the world—or the underworld—is Prince Gog?

Satan's Impersonations of the Kings of the Earth

In the NIV translation of Isaiah 14:12-15 there is a classic text that not a few would consider to be an apt entry for Satan's Curriculum Vitae! It goes like this:

*How you have fallen from heaven, O morning star, son of the dawn! You have been cast down to the earth, you who once laid low the nations! You said in your heart, "I will ascend to heaven; I will raise my throne above the stars of God; I will sit enthroned on the mount of assembly, **on the utmost heights of the sacred mountain**. I will ascend above the tops of the clouds; I will make myself like the Most High." But you are brought down to the grave, to the depths of the pit* (emphasis added).

And the New Living Testament translates the same four verses in the following fashion:

*How you are fallen from heaven, O shining star, son of the morning! You have been thrown down to the earth, you who destroyed the nations of the world. For you said to yourself, "I will ascend to heaven and set my throne above God's stars. **I will preside on the mountain of the gods far away in the north**. I will climb to the highest heavens and be like the Most High." But instead, you will be brought down to the place of the dead, down to its lowest depths* (emphasis added).

For comparison I have bolded both renditions where they again—as in Psalm 48—referred to the "sides of the north." And we're back once more to this sacred mountain which NIV called Mt. Zaphon to show its relationship with "north," but for which we have seen an even clearer linkage with Mount Saphon of Ugarit and the undeniable seat of the Canaanites' cult of Baal worship. However, this time, in *both* Isaiah 14 translations of the Tempter's tragic tumble, that evil "mountain of the north" as it were, also reflects a clear-cut identity with the devil himself.[7]

Most all serious students of Scripture recognize Isaiah 14 to be a metaphoric analogy of Satan in person, presenting the scenario of his being cast out of heaven in the primordial dim, distant eons of time. But when we backtrack to verse 4 of this very chapter, we see that this scenario likewise doubled as discourse with an alternate eye on good old, bad old Nebuchadnezzar of Babylon: "*You will take up this taunt against the king of Babylon: How the oppressor has come to an end!"*

And the entirety of the damning condemnation, doubling for both the king of Babylon as well as the prince of demons personified follows on from verse 4 above. I suggest you do yourself a favor and thoroughly review the whole of the chapter. Researching yesterday for what's going on today as we brace ourselves for tomorrow is hardly a waste of your time!

But if the King of Babylon was a bona fide figure of the devil's double, an added irony is that on at least one occasion, God incredibly labels Nebuchadnezzar as: *"my servant, King of Babylon"*[8] when he sent a message through the prophet Jeremiah that he planned to use sinister old Nebbie to eventually execute God's wrath upon Egypt! Awesome—but invaluable for us to perceive the Almighty's omnipotent view of all *the nations* from ancient times up until this very day!

It was a most similar despot of darkness, Josef Stalin, who coined the term "useful fools" in application of the same principle of manipulating unsuspecting political pawns as if on his personal chess board. The difference: the Almighty has a sovereign right to strike judgment on rapacious rogues who are only too willing to walk into their own traps. Politicians don't have that right, but sadly they do it anyway—at least for the short term!

And then there's one more protégé reflecting the King of Babylon cum Satan. In Chapter 28 of Ezekiel we have another nearly identical representation of the Prince of the Pit in a prophecy against the evil, arrogant, greedy and ruthless tyrant, the King of Tyre. Again it's worth your time to probe the whole chapter, but I will highlight only verses 13 through 17 for now:

You were in Eden, the garden of God; *every precious stone adorned you: ruby, topaz and emerald, chrysolite, onyx and jasper, sapphire, turquoise and beryl. Your settings and mountings were made of gold; on the day you were created they were* *prepared. You were anointed as a guardian cherub, for so I or-dained you. You were on the holy mount of God; you walked among the fiery stones. You were blameless in your ways from the day you were created till wickedness was found in you. Through your widespread trade you were filled with violence, and you sinned. So I drove you in disgrace from the mount of God, and I expelled you, O guardian cherub, from among the fiery stones. Your heart became proud on account of your beauty, and you corrupted your wisdom because of your splendor.* **So I threw you to the earth***; I made a spectacle of you before kings* (emphasis added).

Since when was the King of Tyre tooling around in the terraces of the Garden of God? Or getting kicked off one of the earliest Creation space shuttles? Here we go again! That was the legless lizard who taunted our mama Eve in Genesis 3, remember? The Scriptures take legitimate license to equate and create a living metaphor with the kings of the nations to personify old Snake Eyes of Eden. All you have to do to get your picture taken with the likes of Lucifer is to pretend to be God!

Wooed by the Nations, but Woe Unto Israel

So why not add Prince Gog to the photogenic pretenders in the parade of the kings of the earth that vie to supplement the godhead? So may I suggest that when Ezekiel prophesies:

This is what the Sovereign LORD says: **I am against you, O Gog, chief prince of Meshech** *and Tubal. I will turn you around, put hooks in your jaws and bring you out with your whole army—your horses, your horsemen fully armed, and a great horde with large and small shields, all of them bran-dishing their swords.* **Persia, Cush and Put will be with them,** *all with shields and helmets, also Gomer with all its troops, and Beth Togarmah from the far north with all its troops—the many nations with you* (emphasis added).[9]

it may not necessarily refer to a secular Russia—or an increasingly secular America for that matter—that gets the nod from God to head the charge. But it is rather Satan incarnate to lead the pack which includes Persia (i.e. Iran and the Ayatollahs), Cush (i.e. Sudan of Darfur infamy) and Put (i.e. Colonel Kaddafi's Libya no less) and *"many nations with (him)."*

So how do Iraq, Syria, Lebanon, Saudi Arabia, Jordan, and Egypt fit in? Go figure. Personally I question that "infidel" Russia has the religious qualifications to head up such a "prayerful" parade of the "faithful" enemies of the Beautiful Land![10] So why not let Gog be Gog?

This is *not* to say that Russia may not be somewhat involved. They well may be along with all *the nations*. But I suggest on the basis of an abundance of wannabe princes, Isaiah 14, Ezekiel 28, and some 20 references to a satanically symbolized *north* featuring a paganist *Zaphon*, the "sacred" mountain of the gods, the headship of the coalition might just be a tad higher than a mere humanistic entity.

Little old Czarist cum Communist Russia will certainly have to line up and take her otherwise divinely ordered lumps of judgment with the rest of *the nations*, each according to his own measure of arrogance and rebellion against the King of the Universe. But the final battle to once and for all destroy Israel is far too important to the dominion of darkness to let a non-Islamic novice like the Soviets head the troops!

But how did Russia cop all that reputation of ill repute in the first place? Well, in the good old days—sort of—the linguistic root of "Russia" is *Ros* or *Rus*. At the same time, the Hebrew word for "head" is *Rosh*. Is there a relationship? Maybe? Maybe not! Possibly it was just a bad guess!

So it may be a bit presumptuous to unilaterally give Lenin and lads a few extra political smacks for their seemingly flawed economic policies! Abba will take care of all that sort of thing, as well as a few other universal measurements like how the various nations have been economically programmed to worship their wealth! It all boils down to idolatry anyway, doesn't it?

In summary, this whole thing is not about the will and wisdom of humanistic kings, but about the eternal struggle between the King of the Universe and His adversary from the beginning of time.

So having established that much, let's now move on to see how some of those others among *the nations* have been faring over the millennia in their practice to "play God."

---

[1] Megiddo is on the ancient trade and invasion route through the Jezreel Valley from the north leading south to Jerusalem and beyond. *Armageddon* is a contraction from the Hebrew word *Har* (mountain) joined to Megiddo, i.e. sounding like Armageddon, which is the current site of the ruins of King Solomon's central fortress that guarded his ancient kingdom. The fortress was located on a significant rise surveying the Jezreel Valley, hence *"Mount Megiddo."*

[2] 1 Chronicles 5:4

[3] Revelation 20:7b-10a

[4] The Bargylus Mountains, Mount Saphon and Ugarit have multiple references on http://www.Answers.com

[5] See Joshua 11:1-14.

[6] See *Britannica Concise Encyclopedia: Ugarit* on http://www. Answers.com

[7] Note that NIV uses a parallel footnote for Psalm 48:2 and Isaiah 14:13, linking *"on the north"* [Hebrew: *zaphon*] with demonic significance to *"heights of Zaphon"* in Psalm 48, and equally reinforcing New Living Testament's rendition of Isaiah 14:13: *"mountain of the gods far away in the north,"* also reflecting satanic association.

[8] Jeremiah 43:10

[9] Ezekiel 38:3-6

[10] See Daniel 11:41

CHAPTER 3

Will the Real Mr. Nineveh Please Stand Up!

If you read my brief Introduction just a few pages back, you'll catch the significance of what this Nineveh issue is all about. If you didn't, I suggest it would be a good idea to do so now.

After the Prophet Jonah's reluctant repent-or-perish preaching expedition to the capital of Assyria, the success rate of repentance was so astounding that it's been a beacon of obedience in the Bible ever since. Even the sometime wicked king of Nineveh got in on the act and personally led the charge for that matter. His orders featured sackcloth for humility and fasting for sincerity that ironically extended even to the barnyard beasts. The fear of God fell upon the faithful with 24-7 petitions to the Almighty—the only One who could ever be able to help.

It has been suggested that the grotesque yellowish appearance of Jonah after a three-day residency within the monster fish, would be enough to move anyone to mend his manners; but regardless, the timely turnaround was a solid commitment, and Nineveh was spared from the destruction that the prophet had predicted. That was Nineveh round one.

Nineveh Round Two

But round two that occurred just under a century and a half later was a bit less cheery. Laced with the long-postponed judgment of Heaven's heavy hand, Nineveh was violently overthrown around 625 BC by a joint effort of the Medes and Babylonians after her ruthless reign of some 130 years of arrogance and heartless cruelty. The Sackcloth Sovereign and subjects had long since defected!

Searching out Nineveh's origins, according to Genesis 10, historian Josephus and others, her founder was arch-tycoon Nimrod—hunter, conqueror, and urban development magnate who at the least oversaw the founding of some eight major settlement centers of civilization. The area became what was eventually known as Mesopotamia under the Ottoman Empire, but which the British renamed Iraq in 1921.

Nineveh today is known as Mosul, a city of some 2 million souls located a bit less than 500 km northwest of ancient Babylon. In spite of earnest efforts by the American international coalition willing to effect a post-Saddam peace, Mosul has been notorious of late for gangland execution-style murders and kidnappings of its Christian minority by the Islamist overlords.[1]

Ancient Nineveh's infamy included more of the same style aggression, brutality and bloodshed—not unlike the macho makeup of Nimrod, her founding father. Obviously, not a great deal has changed after more than three millennia of Middle-Eastern type progress!

More recently, the combined coalition efforts of President G.W. Bush and friends in 2003 once and for all removed the sadistic rule of Saddam Hussein. I noted in passing on my website that there was only one thing worse than this notorious bloodletting dictator and that is anarchy!

In the aftermath of Saddam's departure what had these unfortunate remnant sons of Nimrod inherited? Sunnis, Shi'ites, Kurds—anarchists all! I hate to tar any society with a monolithic brush, but a frightening majority is back to testing out the talents they do best—blatant bloodletting and reinventing the truth!

Not that the overthrow was exactly from a page out of the Almighty's "Must-Do-Today" Diary. Perhaps it was—judgment most often is. But it will be interesting to note what happens to their shiny new "democratic" agenda once the "invaders" leave. It seems that the "democratic" majority likes to see a bit of blood on the streets now and then or else they become nostalgic for the good old days!

Ironically, some seven centuries BC, this is what the Almighty declared over Nineveh through the prophet Nahum:

Woe to the city of blood, full of lies, full of plunder, never without victims!"[2]

But hold on! This chapter is hardly going to be a tirade about the Iraq War, past, present, or future. We're looking instead for a latter-day Mr. Nineveh to present himself. Where is he? Back to the cry of Nahum:

The Lord is good, a refuge in times of trouble. He cares for those who trust in him, but with an overwhelming flood he will make an end of Nineveh; he will pursue his foes into darkness. Whatever they plot against the Lord he will bring to an end; trouble will not come a second time.[3]

Say, that sounds all right! God was back in the business then and is still on "our" side. I keep Him in my pocket for good luck in fact! That wicked Iraq—I mean noxious Nineveh—is in ashes. Nahum says that we won't have to worry about them again! But there's another word coming:

From you, O Nineveh, has one come forth who plots evil against the Lord and counsels wickedness."[4]

Plots evil? Who's this plotting evil against the Lord? Saddam Hussein risen from the dead? If this is supposed to be a parody on the present, it couldn't be a modern like me. I'd never do anything to Him. I've got my own little world to run. He has his; I have mine. Moreover, he's so busy; it's time someone took responsibility for local decisions—like us. Make up a few new rules, like Political Correctness. He's got Galaxies galore to look after. We can look after our own back yard! Sound like humanism?

Nineveh: A Preview of Our Times

Remember back in the Garden of Eden how our first mama Eve got off on the wrong foot by thinking that by picking her own clever path she'd eventually get to be like God? Instead of listening up and doing what He said?

Did you ever think that a more decadent humanity than ancient Nineveh could take over re-defining morality? Rewrite the code? Re-invent truth? Move the goal posts? Call evil good and good evil? While Nineveh's beastly behavior was bloodletting, in today's Western world of financial preoccupation and overindulgence, nothing can be more beastly than our greed. Those who have lived for many days in an impoverished Third World have seen it all from afar—and that from the inside out. If murder is messy, coveting wealth is just as greasy! Both crimes have made the Top Ten of Sinai's tablets of stone.[5]

Ever hear of the purpose driven stock portfolio? What about the purpose driven bank account? Now I don't mean to get into a hassle with our "purpose driven" friends. Some perhaps have been helped much by the phraseology. At least we hope so.

But as a linguist and a Bible Translator, I see some problems. Out of 49 references of "driven" in the Scriptures there is *only one* that has any positive connotation whatsoever, and that is a peg driven into the wall in Isaiah 22:25. And if you read on, that particular peg eventually even happened to fall down!

Driven has to do with driving out populations into deprivation, idolaters into exile, armies into defeat, and demons into the abyss. It's hardly a word that inspires the wayward toward good behavior!

In the 23rd Psalm on the other hand: "*He **leads** me beside the still waters, He restores my soul.*" Heaven *leads* us; humanism *drives* us.

With *purpose* there is no problem. Motivation is a God-thing—or should be. Moreover the motives of men are what Abba is specifically concerned with from the Garden of God on through Nineveh and certainly up to the New World Order.

But whoa! Beware of the purpose driven false prophet, the purpose driven preacher, the purpose driven parliamentarian, the purpose driven investor! It's not the profession, but it's what drives him! If you become aware that the *real* motive happens to be a lust for lucre there will certainly be some pseudo saint cum salesman nearby to organize the driving behind it.

There are mountains more of evil ambitions that link ancient Nineveh with a postmodern and humanistic Western world. Yet in summarizing the categories of evil, there are but few overall groupings from Genesis to Revelation. Idolatry is kowtowing to the wrong god, and the god of the Shi'ites and the Sunnis is hardly the only garden path in town!

The god of vengeance, the god of greed, and the god of self-will are identities we might most easily recognize today. The Hebrew Scriptures label these identical three idolatries in reverse, that is, as a positive cry for mercy instead of vengeance, justice instead of greed, and the righteousness of God instead of the self-will of humanity. And the New Testament holds an umbrella of like definition over the infamous trio as "*the lust of the flesh, the lust of the eyes and the pride of life.*"[6]

The only thing that's changed in over three millennia of mischief is the technology that makes us boast that since we're faster (more arrogance per day), more affluent (less dependent on Abba), and that we are both patriotic and religious-minded (only voting for Christians of course) that the naughtiness of Nineveh is not to be known among us. Sorry!

Moreover, here's a bit more meditation material for our hellenistically modified gurus: Since those mundane murder matters are much underreported by the media, they are hard to prove. But in comparing the bloodletting from the pathways of ancient

Nineveh or even the streets of today's Baghdad, we are advised that the monthly body count runs just as high or higher in most American urban gangland crossfire than it does on the monthly average in the current Iraqi war zone!

But wait a minute! Certainly gangland gunfire is hardly manna from heaven, but is this truly at the top of the transgressions typifying America's misbehavior? Before I started this endeavor, I read entirely through the sixteen Hebrew prophets again for a refresher course, and—second to Baal bowing—I noted a recurring charge against Israel was "shedding of innocent blood" in general, and doing so in the streets of Jerusalem in particular.[7] Now with a tad of reflection, this sounded a mite strange since I didn't think Jerusalem had as much of that kind of monkey business as did Nineveh, let alone Detroit or Chicago. Wrong again! Perhaps it was not as much with the numbers, but it was over the top in regard to significance! Let's have a look at Luke 13:34:

> *O Jerusalem, Jerusalem, you who kill the prophets and stone those sent to you, how often I have longed to gather your children together, as a hen gathers her chicks under her wings, but you were not willing!*

And shall we then try Matthew 23:35-36:

> *And so upon you will come all the righteous blood that has been shed on earth, from the blood of righteous Abel to the blood of Zechariah son of Berekiah, whom you murdered between the temple and the altar. I tell you the truth; all this will come upon this generation.*

So there you have it! The big boys who pretended to know their Bibles didn't mess around with just any old rascal's blood on the streets of Jerusalem, but went straight to those pesky prophets! Was it real blood, a metaphor—or both? You guess! They were carrying a message from the King of Creation!

But it does bring to mind that website wizard back in Chapter 1 who had undoubtedly been presented with far more prophetic warnings from the Hebrew prophets than his little brain could handle, but his Replacement Theological training still chose to put his nationalistic nature into orbit quite above the Apple of Abba's eye!

And almost as sinister, the blood of the unborn gurgling down the sewers of America, across Europe and Asia, and—God have mercy—even across the secular side of apostate Israel, is far more sadistic than the give-and-take bloodletting[8] of Nineveh in 625 BC. Thus we can chalk up one more menacing import from the ancients. The ghosts of Assyria daily return to haunt us! Shall we call out again for the real Mr. Nineveh to arise?

What was it that Nahum wrote? *"Woe to the city of blood, full of lies, full of plunder, never without victims!"* [9] He also wrote just below that:

> ...*all because of the wanton lust of a harlot, alluring, the mistress of sorceries, who enslaved nations by her prostitution and peoples by her witchcraft. "I am against you," declares the Lord Almighty. "I will lift your skirts over your face. I will show the nations your nakedness and the kingdoms your shame. I will pelt you with filth; I will treat you with contempt and make you a spectacle. All who see you will flee from you and say, 'Nineveh is in ruins—who will mourn for her?' Where can I find anyone to comfort you?"*[10]

You may or may not know that when you find sensually suggestive terms like "prostitute," "prostitution" or "harlot," from the pen of the Hebrew prophets, it is not necessarily—and possibly not at all—the Hellenistic-minded physical involvement that is in focus.

The broader, generic significance of these perverse activities is the Almighty's distress of losing a once professed lover, and not only the flaunting of sexual perversion. Actually the above prophecy applies *even more to the nation*—then and now—than it does to the individual. That sort of sounds like everyone's guilty!

Most simply, prostitution before the eyes of Abba is deserting Him as your first love, and darting off to delights from one of His rivals—like wealth, affluence, prestige, or power! These hidden delicacies of the soul pay in good coin to the "religious" mentality that gets tired of playing second fiddle to serving a sovereign God! Actually the "divorce" rate is quite high!

Zephaniah Also Warned of the Wolves in the Wings

But now let's check out Zephaniah, another Hebrew prophet who made a parallel proclamation upon Nineveh under the mantle of the Almighty:

He will stretch out his hand against the north and destroy Assyria, leaving Nineveh utterly desolate and dry as the desert.[11]

And more:

This is the carefree city that lived in safety. She said to herself, "I am, and there is none besides me." What a ruin she has become, a lair for wild beasts! All who pass by her scoff and shake their fists.[12]

But Zephaniah is hardly blind to the reprobate perversion of his own city, Jerusalem. Having endeavored to first put his own people on notice, he then turned to warn all of Jerusalem's near neighbors, Philistia, Moab, Ammon, Cush, plus one more swipe at Nineveh for closure. For sure he received precious little applause declaring to the home town crowd:

Woe to the city of oppressors, rebellious and defiled! She obeys no one, she accepts no correction. She does not trust in the Lord, she does not draw near to her God. Her officials are roaring lions; her rulers are evening wolves, who leave nothing for the morning.[13]

So back once more to my Introduction at the beginning: I would underline that it was the prophetic message of this tiny book of Nahum to which the Lord had directed my attention last year in Jerusalem and spoke with down-to-earth authority, *"This message is for your next book."*

So here I am with some divine insight from our friend Nahum, along with his sometime professional partner in prophecy, Zephaniah. If their independently recorded duet of doom sounds a bit heavy—written most likely within two decades of one another— it's all for the good.

History Poised to Repeat Itself With Even Worse Ideas

But wait a minute! As our post-sanity generations disintegrate into unprecedented change, who cares about pre-darkness doom, swords, spears, chariot wheels, and Hebrew prophets? We all should!

I hate to burst your Oscar bubble—or some such inane insanity[14]—but with fire breathing, Judeophobic Iran just months away from successful satellite launching potential of an EMP detonation over *anywhere* they don't like, it's time to take Nahum and friends seriously.

The technology of an Electro-Magnetic Pulse devastation has been around for quite a while, but it seems like Western governments don't like to talk about it, and the leftist-loving media certainly wouldn't say boo either. Why, their Islamic jihadist heroes would never think of doing such a mean thing to consolidate their Caliphate! Except that Iran has made some missile launching tests by conversion of the cargo holds of old freighters—of which there are legion—to open into a clandestine long-range missile launcher. The name of the game is to detonate a fair-sized nuclear device some 200 miles *above* the surface (like say Nebraska) that won't kill people—right away anyway!

What it does kill is everything electronic like all manner of electric power, communication, and transportation—except the ox cart! That takes the targeted nation back to the 19th century in technology like trucks and telephones, and further than that in medicine and food distribution. So thousands will not die as they did in 9-11, but millions will eventually like in the plagues of the Dark Ages. Nice guys, these Jihadists, but if they do it for a "good cause" they will be duly rewarded. So far Obama hasn't had much success in talking them out of these kinds of capers, even though they seem to be the best of friends otherwise!

I suggest you check it out on *Wikipedia*,[15] since technology is hardly my purpose in these pages, other than to alert you that the technical stuff on Answers.com will be so much gobbledygook to most of us, except that if the thing is detonated approximately 120 miles above your kitchen sink—not a problem with modern missiles—it will neutralize cell phones, TVs, computers and all your bank's financial data for 1000 miles in every direction. You can't even call your sister 1500 miles away, since your own cell phone won't work. And if the blast occurs 200 miles up, hers won't work either!

Meanwhile, everything that Nahum and Zephaniah said is still there waiting for you in your Bible—right where you left it. Read on! Whoever said that the whistle that was blown for Nineveh was limited to the 7th century BC? Wise old King Solomon didn't: *"Whatever is has already been, and what will be has been before; and God will call the past to account."*[16]

As I read those three chapters of Nahum that night in the Jerusalem Bed & Breakfast, it sounded like the dire scenario he prophesied would certainly do just as well for modern day America! That's not to mention Europe, the UK, Canada, South Africa, and even all the way down to Australia—and whoever else who might refuse to put their nose onto the ground for Mr. Ahmadinejad and colleagues!

But in closing this chapter, I also found in the interim of my research a most moving Introduction for this very book of Nahum in the *Message Bible*, a thoroughly unique and totally relevant translation for today's moral maladies of soul. Its author-translator, Eugene Peterson shakes us from slumber with:

> "The stage of history is large. Larger-than-life figures appear on this stage from time to time, swaggering about, brandishing weapons and money, terrorizing and bullying. These figures are not, as they suppose themselves to be, at the center of the stage—not, in fact, anywhere near the center. But they make a lot of noise and are able to call attention to themselves. They often manage to get a significant number of people watching and even admiring: big nations, huge armies, important people. At any given moment a few superpower nations and their rulers dominate the daily news. Every century a few of these names are left carved on its park benches, marking rather futile, and in retrospect pitiable, attempts at immortality. The danger is that the noise of these pretenders to power will distract us from what is going on quietly at the center of the stage in the person and action of God…"

So once more will the real Mr. Nineveh please stand up—and then perhaps come forward—for prayer!

---

[1] "Iraqi police: Christian killed 'execution-style' in Mosul," Associated Press, The Jerusalem Post, Jan. 17, 2009
[2] Nahum 3:1
[3] Nahum 1:7-9
[4] Nahum 1:11
[5] See Exodus 20:3-17.
[6] 1 John 2:16 KJV
[7] See Deuteronomy 19:13; 1 Kings 24:4; Ezekiel 22:2; 24:6,9; Hosea 4:2-3; Habakkuk 2:12
[8] Leviticus 17:11
[9] Nahum 3:1

10 Nahum 3:4-7

11 Zephaniah 2:13

12 Zephaniah 2:15

13 Zephaniah 3:1-3

14 Albert Einstein has been attributed to having defined insanity as "doing the same things over and over again while expecting different results."

15 http://www.answers.com/Electro%20Magnetic%20Pulse. There are numerous reports, but scrolling down to Wikipedia: *Electromagnetic pulse* provides the researcher with distance charts.

16 Ecclesiastes 3:15

CHAPTER 4

The Best of Babylon

Before we get too far into this chapter, I'd better warn you, there won't be too much good, better, or best coming out of Babylon. Like Nineveh, Babylon was founded by a less than God-honoring Nimrod with its first mention once again in Genesis 10:2. The general area was also known as Shinar, the precise site of the ingenious but ultimately infamous tower of Babel.[1]

The root of the name *babel* signals confusion of communication, since the Lord of all life had been less than impressed with Nimrod's methods to get to the top. As a result, He had divinely imposed some linguistic limitations on the whole massive construction crew. We might say in summary that this presumptuous plan clashed with the Creator's own ideas how best to get to heaven and consequently never even got off the ground!

The major Babylonian influence and culture, however, spanned some 1250 years in all, but as a reigning political superpower her supremacy could be broken down into three short spans of world authority. Hammurabi from 1792 to 1750 BC was probably Babylon's most academic and least belligerent super-boss. Nebuchadnezzar I's tenure of global supremacy lasted a mere 21 years, while Nebuchadnezzar II—the one that lion-defying Daniel knew best—ruled with unquestionably the heaviest hand for 43 years from 605 to 562 BC.

So Babylon's real superpower chiefs held sway for little more than a century collectively, while the remaining years of Babylon's political ups and downs were fought over by the Assyrians, Armenians, Chaldeans, Kassites, and the Elamites. Finally, a very short-tenured King Belshazzar, who happened to see the handwriting on the wall while hosting an orgy, wisened up a wee bit too late we might note. He was assassinated by Darius the Mede that very same night. That happened to be in collusion with the Persians in 539 BC, and a new set of superpower seekers began a sort of "cutthroat" bid for office. Not surprisingly, that has been the only kind of "democratic" electioneering the Middle East ever knew!

Babylon's Ongoing Encore

It goes without saying that the Medes and the Persians messed up Belshazzar's booze party but good! Unfortunately, Babylon's band played on, right up to chapter 18 in the Book of Revelation! We'll touch on this again at the end of the chapter.

I have written considerably more about Babylon's eternal significance in my previous work, *Who Told You That You Were Naked?* that may fill in a gap or two in some of our understanding as we move on. Chapter 2 in that book, *"Hot Line to Heaven"*; Chapter 13, *"Multiplication of Mammon for the Great Divide"*; and Chapter 14, *"All Your Eggs in How Many Baskets?"* are suggested for added reading or review.[2]

The most damning of Babylon's world-wide influence has been her idolatrous anti-God legacy—hence the demonic proliferation to this day. And in a nearly four millennia-long irony, this competitive confrontation with the Creator continues to irk the less than "spooked" of us today.

A neo-Babylonian anti-God mentality masquerades under a Halloween-type guise of the CFR—the Council of Foreign Relations—aka the think tank for the New World Order. We are offered the *treat* of One World Government, complete with Political Correctness and a world free of iniquity, since they have re-written the manual, and there is no such malady as sin anymore!

The trick, on the other hand, is the rug that is pulled out from under the Ancient of Days faster than yesterday's charlatans pulled rabbits from a hat! But the Babylon bonus is, you'll get *both* trick *and* treat, that boils down to neither any good from below, nor any God from above!

From the first mention of Babylon in Genesis 10:2, it pretty well takes the unchallenged kooky kudos award as the demonic capital of the globe—then and now. We'll pick up on the noxious depths of her notoriety as we move down the pages. But if it becomes truly necessary to expose your neighbor's naughtiness, it's always polite to say something nice first. So we'll try.

I concede that it's going to be a bit hard to give a rave review for the domain of the demonic, but I do have one positive report for starters. It's tale in the entirety is in Daniel 4 about King Nebuchadnezzar II's dream.

Now Nebbie was a nuisance when it came to dreams. He had one already in Daniel 2 which troubled him tremendously so he called together the very best in the brain bank of Babylon and had the cheek to tell them he had a miserable dream, but he had forgotten it! So if they would tell him first of all what the dream was, and secondly what it meant, he wouldn't cut their heads off! How nice can you get? Well to make a long story short, prophet Daniel came along and by God's divine intervention he was able to preserve *both ends* of the pickle—both the dream *and* the meaning—and saved the day, including the heads of the court wizards!

But his next dream two chapters later was different. This time he actually remembered what the dream entailed, though he was still at a loss to know what it meant. You guessed it! His brightest lads in the court still didn't have a clue, but this time he didn't have to threaten to pull the plug on the think tank but had sense enough to take a shortcut to Daniel. The dream:

> *These are the visions I saw while lying in my bed: I looked, and there before me stood a tree in the middle of the land. Its height*

was enormous. The tree grew large and strong and its top touched the sky; it was visible to the ends of the earth. Its leaves were beautiful, its fruit abundant, and on it was food for all. Under it the beasts of the field found shelter, and the birds of the air lived in its branches; from it every creature was fed. In the visions I saw while lying in my bed, I looked, and there before me was a messenger, a holy one, coming down from heaven. He called in a loud voice: "Cut down the tree and trim off its branches; strip off its leaves and scatter its fruit. Let the animals flee from under it and the birds from its branches. But let the stump and its roots, bound with iron and bronze, remain in the ground, in the grass of the field. Let him be drenched with the dew of heaven, and let him live with the animals among the plants of the earth. Let his mind be changed from that of a man and let him be given the mind of an animal, till seven times pass by for him."[3]

And with wisdom from the Most High, Daniel gave the King the meaning:

You, O king, are that tree! You have become great and strong; your greatness has grown until it reaches the sky, and your dominion extends to distant parts of the earth. You, O king, saw a messenger, a holy one, coming down from heaven and saying, "Cut down the tree and destroy it, but leave the stump, bound with iron and bronze, in the grass of the field, while its roots remain in the ground. Let him be drenched with the dew of heaven; let him live like the wild animals, until seven times pass by for him." You will be driven away from people and will live with the wild animals; you will eat grass like cattle and be drenched with the dew of heaven. Seven times will pass by for you until you acknowledge that the Most High is sovereign over the kingdoms of men and gives them to anyone he wishes. Therefore, O king, be pleased to accept my advice: Renounce your sins by doing what is right, and your wickedness by being

*kind to the oppressed. It may be that then your prosperity will
continue.*[4]

And the narrative goes on:

*All this happened to King Nebuchadnezzar. Twelve months
later, as the king was walking on the roof of the royal palace of
Babylon, he said, "Is not this the great Babylon I have built as
the royal residence, by my mighty power and for the glory of my
majesty?" The words were still on his lips when a voice came
from heaven, "This is what is decreed for you, King
Nebuchadnezzar: Your royal authority has been taken from you.
You will be driven away from people and will live with the
wild animals; you will eat grass like cattle. Seven times will
pass by for you until you acknowledge that the Most High is
sovereign over the kingdoms of men and gives them to anyone
he wishes." Immediately what had been said about
Nebuchadnezzar was fulfilled. He was driven away from
people and ate grass like cattle. His body was drenched with the
dew of heaven until his hair grew like the feathers of an eagle
and his nails like the claws of a bird.*[5]

And then the best of Babylon—the best thing we can ever
hope to emerge from the demonic domain of the prince of darkness. The king's repentance:

*At the end of that time, I, Nebuchadnezzar, raised my eyes to-
ward heaven, and my sanity was restored. Then I praised the
Most High; I honored and glorified him who lives forever. His
dominion is an eternal dominion; his kingdom endures from
generation to generation. All the peoples of the earth are regarded as nothing. He does as he pleases with the powers of
heaven and the peoples of the earth. No one can hold back his
hand or say to him: "What have you done?" At the same time
that my sanity was restored, my honor and splendor were returned to me for the glory of my kingdom. My advisers and no-*

bles sought me out, and I was restored to my throne and became even greater than before. Now I, Nebuchadnezzar, praise and exalt and glorify the King of heaven, because everything he does is right and all his ways are just. And those who walk in pride he is able to humble.[6]

Not bad, really, but as you may have supposed it didn't last for all that long. But at least we have a glimmer of the authority of the God of the galaxies in that ancient culture of go-it-alone godlessness and good luck for the lack of anything else!

So what else is new?

Abraham's Momentous Move

Well, Abraham was a breath of fresh air to the depravity of his day. He lived in Ur, a suburb in the south of this Babylonian pagan culture of idolatry that dominated the entire area. I have made significant mention of him in chapter one, *"A Man Named Abraham,"* of my previous book, *Where Is the Body?*[7] should you wish to broaden your view of that particular scenario.

In fact Hebrew tradition has it that his father, Terah, probably made and sold idol statues for his sustenance, and young Abe possibly even worked for his dad in the shop. More tradition in numerically linking the longevity of Noah to young Abram as he was known in his former years, suggests that their life spans must have certainly overlapped. Moreover, the younger man most possibly learned a few clues of celestial boat building from Noah himself, along with down-to-earth faith from a great mentor who knew God personally.

Anyway the rest of Abraham's patriarchic life begins in Genesis 12:1-5:

The Lord had said to Abram, "Leave your country, your people and your father's household and go to the land I will show you. I will make you into a great nation and I will bless you; I will make your name great, and you will be a blessing. I will bless those who bless you, and whoever curses you I will curse; and all peoples on earth will be blessed through you." So Abram left, as the Lord had told him; and Lot went with him. Abram was seventy-five years old when he set out from Haran. He took his wife Sarai, his nephew Lot, all the possessions they had accumulated and the people they had acquired in Haran, and they set out for the land of Canaan, and they arrived there.

Please permit me at this point to backtrack once more—this time with one added "best" for Babylon, which in my normal pattern of word-play I find it most hard to resist. As the Almighty might well have said to Abram, *"Son, this place is so full of demons that you'd **best** get out of here"*—another usage of "best" that obliquely fits the picture!" And get out of there, he did.

As I have just recommended a review on *"A Man Called Abraham"* from my previous book, it needs no repetition here except to focus on perhaps the primary purpose for moving Abraham and his entire entourage out of Ur of Babylon. The initial leg was first to Canaan, but ultimately on up to Jerusalem. And why Jerusalem? Was there a specific reason? Indeed there was!

The First Glimpse of the Big Picture

The Torah—the five books of Moses—refers to the offspring of Abraham, Isaac, and Jacob as the "Children of Israel." Fathering a family of redemption was one thing while the specific site of their new location was yet another. Most of my readers would know of the Hebrews' migration to Egypt in the dire days of famine, and their eventual role of being cast into slavery by their Egyptian masters. And you would also know of the call of Moses to lead them back to the Land of Promise. But would you know the specific designation of *where* Moses was to finally lead them to culminate the wilderness journey of 40 years and more than a million migrants?

Well it wasn't Canaan. Abba had other long-term plans for the

Canaanites, that is, scattering and judgment. And it wasn't Israel! Jacob's boundaries—and the name of the land *within* those boundaries—was yet to be established by Joshua on their return trek from Egyptian bondage. And it was anything but "Palestine"—a fictitious name invented by Roman Emperor Hadrian some five or six centuries after the disappearance of the Philistines as a race. Sadly, the kings of the earth—aka anti-Semites then and now—gloried in this memorial to Goliath and friends, and *Palestine* remains a bogus description of the land to this day.[8]

But we *can* find the God-designated location of the place where Moses was to lead the Family of Redemption noted some 20 times in the book of Deuteronomy:

> *But you are to seek the place the Lord your God will choose from among all your tribes to put his Name there for his dwelling. To that place you must go...*[9]

So there you have it. Satan initially established his demonic headquarters in Babylon. It was his stronghold of influence upon *the nations*, and his culture of confusion for control over all emerging civilizations in that broad proximity between the Tigris and Euphrates Rivers.[10]

While on the other hand, the King of the Universe, in sending His chosen Abraham out to plant the family of Redemption, chose Jerusalem instead as His own eternal seat of authority to confront and, in the end, overthrow his archenemy in idolatrous Babylon.

In former days, God had sent His pioneer Abraham—at the time—to little known Mount Moriah for a trial run on a seemingly mindless, paganized, and equally abhorrent human sacrifice of his only son Isaac. It turned out that Isaac was but a prototype of the real run in days to come. God said in essence to Abraham, *"See the ram over there caught in the undergrowth; use him for the offering. In an appointed time, I'll provide my own sacrifice."*[11]

Mt. Moriah turned out to be the identical Mount Calvary of death and resurrection renown—an extended ridge on the very

Temple Mount—*Har HaBayit* in Hebrew—where the treasured temple of Solomon once stood supreme in Jerusalem.

But the fine tuning of God's mention of "the place" 20 times in the Book of Deuteronomy, is not so much the *name* of the place, but its *purpose.* Indeed, it was called Jerusalem, Mount Zion, or Har HaBayit, but the significance of any of these names is a *place of polarity* to counter the demonic defiance of godlessness against the King of the Universe!

So in a counter move—but hardly the final one—who was it that attacked and destroyed Jerusalem in 586 BC? The Babylonians, of course!

Jeremiah both laments but then adds the Almighty's promise in 50:17-19:

> *Israel is a scattered flock that lions have chased away. The first to devour him was the king of Assyria; the last to crush his bones was Nebuchadnezzar king of Babylon. Therefore this is what the Lord Almighty, the God of Israel, says: "I will punish the king of Babylon and his land as I punished the king of Assyria. But I will bring Israel back to his own pasture and he will graze on Carmel and Bashan; his appetite will be satisfied on the hills of Ephraim and Gilead."*

The Temple Mount and Her Untenable Tenants

The temple was eventually rebuilt in 515 BC, but this time it was the Romans who in due course also took that one out in 70 AD. And the forlorn and forsaken Jews—forsaken by *the nations* we might note—were scattered to the ends of the earth. But it was not without some 85 biblical promises from the prophets of the Most High that they would one day return—forever. One of the classic ones is in Amos 9:14-15:

> *And I will bring again the captivity of my people of Israel, and they shall build the waste cities, and inhabit [them]; and they*

44

shall plant vineyards, and drink the wine thereof; they shall also make gardens, and eat the fruit of them. And I will plant them upon their land, and they shall no more be pulled up out of their land which I have given them, saith the LORD thy God.

Very interesting! As the multi-god Babylonian dominance of the Middle East eventually made a presumably arbitrary selection (we seriously doubt a democratic election), *Illat,* the once-upon-a-time moon-god,[12] with a series of inter-tribal wars and buckets of bloodshed ultimately crystallized into a modified "monotheism." And Islam evolved from early in the 7th century AD.

Islam bore the more or less self-absorbed idea that its warmed over wisdom was so great that Jews and Christians alike would crawl all over themselves to get into the blessings (especially the women!). But when the infidels were such ingrates and it didn't happen, the venom became so fiery—violence being a rare reaction in Babylon's by-products anyway!—that Jews shot to the top of Mecca's hit list for forever and a day. And the less than impressed Christians came in second only because in the Islamic worldview there can be absolutely nothing worse than the Jew! Using a phrase the Hebrew writers frequently penned to signal a permanence of one circumstance or another: and the hatred remains *"to this day."*

The abridged version of the deteriorating relationship is that not one but two mosques appeared over the ruins of Israel's First and Second Temples on the sacred Temple Mount just shortly after 700 AD, and to again repeat that biblical phrase of longevity, these mosques likewise remain there *"to this day."*

This fictional fracas of who was first also requires one additional footnote, which Yasser Arafat and like-minded liquidators quoted incessantly: "The Jews claim that they once had a Temple on this place, but there is no historical evidence to substantiate this ridiculous claim."

Jerusalem happens to be unique as one of the few major cities of the globe—if not the *only* one—that has no above ground waterway coursing within her boundaries. She does have a sizeable underground aquifer that could one day fall into the fulfillment of Ezekiel's prophecy in his Chapter 47, but no real rivers except for a different variety: The flow of fabrication from a Babylon-styled mindset and her centuries later Islamic offspring is an unabated torrent of untruth to undermine Israel and her eternal title to the Holy City.

The kings of *the nations*, the media mind-benders, the cartels of crude oil, and the financiers of far-flung investments, would each have us believe that the world's woes can best be observed from their personal perspectives—complete with their own self-serving solutions.

Sorry, but I am here to declare that all ills from global finance, petro-production, media sensationalism, anti-Semitism, Islam, and a multitude of die-hard divisions all have their roots—at least in some limited linkage—with the God-question: "Who *does* own the Temple Mount?"

Two Reasons for Everything— A Good Reason and the Real Reason

There are several books or articles that have come out recently to underscore what I have just declared above.

A recent article in the *Jerusalem Post* by Ruthie Blum Leibowitz, "*It's Religion Stupid!*"[13] presents an interview with author Roberta Green-Ahmanson whose latest title is: *Blind Spot: When Journalists Don't Get Religion.*[14] Both the article and the book see the true scenario. And another *Post* article entitled "Lewis: Conflict Seen as Mainly Religious" from 17 February 2009 by Etgar Lefkovits presents the parallel insights of Bernard Lewis, Professor Emeritus of Princeton University in an article that caught even a bit more of the sunrise of reality.[15] Lewis has written an impressive number of volumes on insights into the Middle East religious mind that historians and scholars are much more apt to catch than journalists, financiers, and political adventurers.

To the journalist devoid of the awareness of a God who guides the galaxies, nothing could be more "god-like" than the personal scoop of a great story. The pride of life parades its ladder of prestige from pauper up to prince. The eye of greed sees no greater god than the gold in his vault. And the black gold from the Persian Gulf to the Gulf of Mexico carries its own keys to power and success.

The gods of Babylon—and they are legion—each carry their glitter of a personal goal. And if we have never seen anything higher—and even deny there could be anything higher—we are hard put to fairly interpret any truth. But to stumble upon the moment of truth that there is a divinely ordered polarity between the bubble of Babylon and the bedrock confidence in a *"Thus saith the Lord"* makes all else chincy-cheap.

Indeed, it's religion stupid! It is a watershed of whether one bets on bubbles over against a personal intimacy with the Divine.

Ah! Babylon and her mortals—then no different than now! There are those who persist in worshipping her gods from crude castings of yesteryear to the cleverness of control through cyberspace in our time. Or alternately, is it Jerusalem and the God who actually created her stones and was even on hand—a bit incognito, perhaps—at the coronation of Jerusalem's eternal King?

He designed stones of personal brokenness:

Everyone who falls on that stone will be broken to pieces, but he on whom it falls will be crushed. [16]

He programmed Stones that speak:

"I tell you,' he replied, 'if they keep quiet, the stones will cry out.'" [17]

And rough-cut Stones that cause stumbling:

...and he will be a sanctuary; but for both houses of Israel he

will be a stone that causes men to stumble and a rock that makes them fall. And for the people of Jerusalem he will be a trap and a snare.[18]

He engineered living Stones to build a new kind of temple:

In him the whole building is joined together and rises to become a holy temple in the Lord. And in him you too are being built together to become a dwelling in which God lives by his Spirit.[19]

And tallest of all, the Rock that is higher than I:

From the ends of the earth I call to you, I call as my heart grows faint; lead me to the rock that is higher than I.[20]

And the Ancient of Days even attended the unique crowning of her King:

The chief priests of the Jews protested to Pilate, "Do not write 'The King of the Jews,' but that this man claimed to be king of the Jews." Pilate answered, "What I have written, I have written."[21]

The Curtain Falls on Babylon

Finally, there are a few more verses in the Good Book to sign off with Babylon. But before the eulogies, may we review that it was all over for Babylon I in 539 BC, overthrown by Darius the Mede as recorded in Daniel 5:30.

Sit in silence, go into darkness, Daughter of the Babylonians; no more will you be called queen of kingdoms.[22]

Babylon, the jewel of kingdoms, the glory of the Babylonians' pride, will be overthrown by God like Sodom and Gomorrah.[23]

Babylon II, however, is currently overrunning the end-of-days stage of destiny, sporting a sort of deadly wound that somehow rose up from the ashes.[24] Nevertheless, she yet awaits the "appointed time" to once and for all, finally meet her Maker.

With a mighty voice he shouted: "Fallen! Fallen is Babylon the Great! She has become a home for demons and a haunt for every evil spirit, a haunt for every unclean and detestable bird."[25]

Therefore in one day her plagues will overtake her: death, mourning and famine. She will be consumed by fire, for mighty is the Lord God who judges her. When the kings of the earth who committed adultery with her and shared her luxury see the smoke of her burning, they will weep and mourn over her. Terrified at her torment, they will stand far off and cry: "Woe! Woe, O great city, O Babylon, city of power! In one hour your doom has come!"[26]

Then a mighty angel picked up a boulder the size of a large millstone and threw it into the sea, and said: "With such violence the great city of Babylon will be thrown down, never to be found again."[27]

Chasing after idols always was and ever will be—from past tense to post modern—a less than sparkling seduction!

[1] See Genesis 11:1-9
[2] Victor Schlatter, *Who Told You that You Were Naked?* (Shippensburg, PA: Destiny Image Publishers, 2006).
[3] Daniel 4:10-16
[4] Daniel 4: 22-27.
[5] Daniel 4:28-33.
[6] Daniel 4:34-37.
[7] Victor Schlatter, *Where Is the Body?* (Shippensburg, PA: Destiny Image Publishers, 1999). Chapter 2, *"A Man Called Abraham."*
[8] In 132AD, after a 2nd sacking of Jerusalem in just over 60 years, out of anti-Jewish rage, Emperor Hadrian renamed Judea, *Falistina,* in deference to the former Philistines, and the misnomer remained across history.
[9] Deuteronomy 12:5, with like references in Deut. 12:11, 18, 21, 26 and 15 similar references throughout Deuteronomy.

10 Genesis 2:14 is most frequently cited by biblical researchers and others as the cradle of civilization.

11 See the full account in Gen 22:1-19.

12 Check out "Illat the moon god" on http://www.Answers.com ; also see Victor Schlatter, *Who Told You that You Were Naked* ? (Shippensburg, PA: Destiny Image Publishers, 2006), Endnote 1, p.142.

13http://www.jpost.com/servlet/Satellite?cid=1231950850527&pagename=JPost%2FJPArticle%2FShowFull

14 Roberta Green Ahmanson, *Blind Spot: When Journalists Don't Get Religion*, (Oxford University Press, by Paul Marshall, Lela Gilbert, and Roberta Green-Ahmanson, Nov. 2008)

15http://www.jpost.com/servlet/Satellite?cid=1233304811420&pagename=JPost%2FJPArticle%2FShowFull

16 Luke 20:18

17 Luke 19:40.

18 Isaiah 8:14.

19 See all of Ephesians 2:19-22.

20 Psalm 61:2.

21 John 19:21-22

22 Isaiah 47:5

23 Isaiah 13:19

24 See Revelation 13:3, 13:12 &13:14b; also see Victor Schlatter, *Who Told You That You Were Naked?*, (Shippensburg, PA: Destiny Image Publishers, 2006). Chapter 14, *All Your Eggs in How Many Baskets?*

25 Revelation 18:2

26 Revelation 18:8-10

27 Revelation 18:21

CHAPTER 5

The Precedent of Persia

Now we just finished off with how Darius the Mede jammed the genies of Babylon (aka demons) back into their bottle and corked it for good back in 539 BC. Unfortunately the liberal loonies of the latter days messed around and ridiculously removed the cork once more with some post-Almighty postulations about a New World Order; read: Neo-Babylonian blasphemy. But that's for a bit later.

At the moment, however, we need to clarify that a daunting Darius was only acting in tandem with a bit more prestigious Cyrus the Great, the sovereign potentate of Persia at the time.

A Gentile King Is Privy to the Plan for Jerusalem

Now when we use the term "precedent" for Persia, we are suggesting that they are a step ahead of something or someone else. That *someone else* happens to be *the nations*, and the *someone* who is a bit in the forefront, is good old Cyrus himself. This is what God said of him in Isaiah:

> The LORD who says of Cyrus, "*He is my **shepherd** and will accomplish all that I please"; he will say of Jerusalem, "Let it be rebuilt," and of the temple, "Let its foundations be laid."*

> *This is what the Lord says to his **anointed**, to Cyrus, whose right hand I take hold of to subdue nations before him and to strip kings of their armor, to open doors before him so that gates will not be shut.*[1]

Moreover Persia had become the superpower of the day, and Cyrus was the king who called the shots. And superpowers are called superpowers because their neighboring nations have to pretty much go along with what they say. So look what Cyrus said in Ezra 1:1-3:

> *In the first year of Cyrus king of Persia, in order to fulfill the word of the Lord spoken by Jeremiah, the Lord moved the heart of Cyrus king of Persia to make a proclamation throughout his realm and to put it in writing: This is what Cyrus king of Persia says: "The Lord, the God of heaven, has given me all the kingdoms of the earth and he has appointed me to build a temple for him at Jerusalem in Judah. Anyone of his people among you—may his God be with him, and let him go up to Jerusalem in Judah and build the temple of the Lord, the God of Israel, the God who is in Jerusalem."*

Now why in the world would a pagan king say something like that when nations in general and superpowers in particular are not a little anti-Semitic and have this thing about dividing up Jerusalem like a piece of non-Kosher pizza—with a slice for every Amalekite and his brother.

I told you that Persia did set a precedent, didn't I? First of all, he *wasn't* a pagan king. A pagan is someone who neither knows nor fears the Almighty. And good old Cyrus must have bumped into the Lord of Hosts somewhere in his travels, and consequently was duly impressed. Maybe it was through Daniel, since there were three biblical mentions of King Cyrus in Isaiah plus a couple more in 2 Chronicles, and Daniel seemed to be around during those days. He did get to know a few of these king types along the way and did carry a positive reflection to people in high places wherever he went. That's not a bad precedent for Daniel either, except that's what we all ought to be doing in a reflection of the King of glory.

Or perhaps Cyrus discovered the treasure trove of the Genesis 12:3 promise somewhere that gave him a few clues on which side his eternal bread was to be buttered. That is what God declared to Abraham—as well as all the rest of us—in regard to the Family of Promise he was to father:

I will bless those who bless you, and whoever curses you I will curse; and all peoples on earth will be blessed through you.

So Cyrus turned out to be appropriately clued-in for a so-called "pagan king." Not even half the churches in America are on to that verse for what it ought to mean to them and their prayer time!

Anyway it definitely earned him some points with the King of the Universe who called Cyrus His "shepherd" and His "anointed" as in the opening quotations from Isaiah above. The Almighty also held his right hand to break down bronze gates and all sorts of magnificent matters. It's amazing what Abba does for those who *really* get on His side and stay there!

So that's how Persia got a bit of a celestial head start in those early days of superpower surfing. It's obvious, therefore, that the anti-Semitic global societies of today's Hellenist godless-wonders could use a tad of their own God-connection as well. Even the disappointingly downgraded president Ahmadinejad of the present Persia—aka Iran—ought to be picking up a few lessons from the good old days. Shortsighted he is, sad if not a bit stupid!

Consequences of Blessing or Cursing His Chosen People

But it may come as a bitter bombshell, not only to Ahmadinejad but to all the otherwise blustering "religious" types—including not a few Christians—that the real significance of the Genesis 12:3 blessing of Israel is hardly Jew worship.

It should be noted that if you ever go to Tel Aviv—or Texas for that matter—not all Jews still want to be Jews and are looking for the front, side, or back door to get out. In Numbers 16, one Korah along with 250 families—Hebrews all—reckoned they had thought up a better way to run the universe, and the earth opened up and swallowed the lot. Frightening!

And then there are some of the Chosen Family who are fed up with the world hating them,[2] and who loathe that they were born Jews. These also would be happy to get out. But in a quite similar but reversed vein, there are Gentiles from *the nations* from here to China who are eager to be grafted into the family.[3] Possibly some of these even have a few Hebraic genes from generations back. Except for Abba, who knows?

But the focus of Genesis 12:3 is not about ethnicity but about God's purpose. If Abba chose the Jews to be His instruments for world redemption, don't mess up His tool kit! So if you're born into that Abrahamic tool kit, or if you're grafted in, or if you don't have a clue how you happen to be empathetically among them—the bottom line is that if God can save the likes of *any* of the clan, He can do it for anyone else He chooses. So you can relax!

Therefore, the promise in Genesis 12:3 is not about who, who, who or Jew, Jew, Jew. It's about Abba's protective defensiveness over anyone else interfering with his redemptive plan, plan, plan and points only to God, God, God. So to Mr. Ahmadinejad— whose fiery bluster could well nominate his whole nation for entry into the past tense, my advice is—watch it!

Another Anti-Semite in the Wrong Place at the Wrong Time

Unfortunately biblical Persia also had one other pre-Ayatollah attack from the kingdom of quality carpets. Another Jew hater by the name of Haman crept into the picture and nearly obliterated all the Jews of the Persian Empire back in the days of Queen Esther. Where do these jealous jokers come from anyway?

We find all of this in the book of Esther at the time of King Ahasuerus who came along some 50 years after our good friend Cyrus. He is also called Xerxes in NIV and a number of English translations, which a bit of research explains as being his *real* name, while Ahasuerus was simply the title used in Persia to identify a king.

Somehow the title *Ahasuerus* seems to have a much more soothing ring to it than the modern Ayatollah tag. If you have trouble pronouncing Xerxes don't use the NIV for reading Esther, but maybe the New King James. Regardless, the story of Queen Esther is a beauty—as she also was—and she was also the newly chosen wife of King X which is another way of handling the funny spelling. However, I don't want to get into that either, but suggest you look it up and read it for yourself in whatever translation you use.

However, we must talk about Haman. He was one of those early "snake-oil" salesmen from days of yore, but in spite of that, he had somehow impressed King Xerxes to the point of flogging top kudos in the kingdom. The bitter truth is that he was hardly a Hebrew-heralding descendant of Cyrus, but a bitter Jew-hater from the offspring of Amalek. He is identified in Esther 3:1 as an Agagite, and Agag had been an Amalekite king supposedly to have been destroyed by King Saul but wasn't.[4]

Now this has far more significance than a family feud or an ancient tribal tiff. Amalek was the grandson of Esau who in scriptural sequence, shows us—along with Uncle Ishmael—an unbridgeable divide in the Family of Promise between those who chose to follow the faith of founding father Abraham, and those who evoked the pre-Abrahamic venom of Cain. This is *not* to say that individual members from the offspring of those two earlier family schisms of jealous hatred (i.e. Ishmael and Esau) cannot be forgiven and redeemed by the Eternal Atonement, but Scripture is clear that there is a specific and ongoing generational spiritual battle that needs to be recognized, confronted, and conquered.

Amalek is a cover euphemism used by the Jews to this very day to depict the satanic spiritual forces rooted from antiquity to destroy them as a people. Abundantly clear biblical warnings are given in Exodus 17:8-16 that go quite beyond human hatred, exposing the demonic essence of Amalek:

> *Then the Lord said to Moses, "Write this on a scroll as something to be remembered and make sure that Joshua hears it, because I will completely blot out the memory of Amalek from under heaven." Moses built an altar and called it The Lord is my Banner. He said, "Because a hand was lifted up against the throne of the Lord.5 The Lord will be at war against the Amalekites from generation to generation."6*

A second reinforcing reference is Deuteronomy 25:17-19:

> *Remember what the Amalekites did to you along the way when you came out of Egypt. When you were weary and worn out, they met you on your journey and cut off all who were lagging behind; they had no fear of God. When the Lord your God gives you rest from all the enemies around you in the land he is giving you to possess as an inheritance, you shall blot out the memory of Amalek from under heaven. Do not forget!*

Thus we find Haman, an Amalekite of descending generations of hatred, oozing into an otherwise pro-Israel superpower of ancient times. In fact it was the *only* pro-Israel superpower of any significant historical memory.

So ancient Persia seems to kind of remind us of yesterday's America. There were great saints like Cyrus but never without a prickly Haman or two to mess up the music.

Anti-Semitism Brings Judgment

No serious Bible believer can deny that the Scriptures cry out loud and clear that the manner in which any nation treats the Jews—call it Abba's Pilot Project of Redemption if you like—is the code of "justice" they will receive in kind at the final judgment call of the King of the Universe. Consider the well-known separation of the "pearls from the plastic" in Matthew 25:31-45: *"The King will reply, 'I tell you the truth, whatever you did for one of the least of these brothers of mine, you did for me.'"* [7]

May we be advised that the king in question is obviously Jewish, but it's neither King David nor King Solomon, and hardly King James!

History cries out as well. There was Nazi Germany whose industrial cities were flattened to near oblivion in the final days of WWII. A repentant nation and a total change of the guard brought restoration and relief.

Then there was the Pharaoh of Egypt who "knew not Joseph" and the king's brutal taskmasters. Rose-colored history glasses may perhaps treat them a mite better in the theatrical presentations of the *Ten Plagues of Egypt* as they might be imagined today. But it was an anguished judgment upon the ancients that meted out their misery and pain, and hardly the fickle memoirs of a staged history some three millennia after the fact.

In passing we have touched on the Assyrians and the Babylonians not to mention the Ammonites, the Moabites, the Edomites, and the Philistines. The latter have disappeared entirely as a people, while the former three have morphed into third class citizenry of the Arab world. *"Do not be deceived: God cannot be mocked. A man reaps what he sows."* [8] And this is doubly true when the Almighty sets out with His plans already on the drawing board.

Go ahead and corrupt your own life and environs to the highest heaven. Your day in the dock can wait! But woe unto the man or woman who lays a hand against the divine blueprint of the Great Beyond! We must all know of a few stubborn souls who are no longer with us since their efforts ran counter to what the Creator had planned, and therefore were not conducive to longevity! We hesitate saying it, we don't even like to think about it, but the facts are on the ground and we quietly recognize it when we see it:

He who is often rebuked, and hardens his neck, Will suddenly be destroyed, and that without remedy. [9]

The bottom line, there's a price to be paid for messing with the Jew, and particularly so if your beef is with his birthright! King Cyrus was one of the few global giants who had no problems.

How America Fares for the Future

Moreover, most of America's Bible believers know this well. And that's why there is such a high percentage of support for Israel from the Americans. May we hark back once more to Ruthie Blum Leibowitz's *Jerusalem Post* article:"It's Religion Stupid." Those less than lucid politicians and journalists keep gurgling that American support of Israel is because of the Jewish lobby in Washington. Not so! It's really because of what so many Americans have seen in their Bibles!

Unfortunately, not too many of our Bible reading Cyrus types in the USA are occupying the inner-sanctum of the White House and nearby buildings. Certainly there are a few within the corridors of power up to a point, but much like in the days of ancient Israel's idolatrous downside, there are far too many other buddies of Baal[10] also in town to deflect American hearts and eyes away from the end of days drawing board of the ages. These Baals that bow to quite another god from the One that Cyrus regarded, are flashing their finest lures in the way of temptation to look to Israel's neighbors to the north, south, and east of Israel.

On the one hand they evoke tears of compassionate pity to the penniless plight of Israel's surrounding minions, whose fictitious tales of woe once again curse Israel, the world's oldest scapegoat. It seems that the masters of mercy, appear not to tally that the billions of aid given globally to Israel's poverty stricken neighbors goes largely to bombs and bullets instead of bread. Moreover, other of these pitiful paupers do happen to be sitting on a fair bit of crude oil!

And in the meanwhile, the influential Baals of D.C. point out the plums of prosperity and power, of which for the purposes of political gain, there is precious little difference.

So as the economies of the globe continue to plummet and the bankruptcies of the battered continue to mount, the premier idolatry of the ages continues to greedily grasp for a glitter that neither belongs to them nor ever will.

Back to the oil gods: OPEC is probably the shiniest Baal on the block. No one can teach us how to worship the Riyal[11] any better than the Saudis. But we're a God-fearing nation—started out that way at least—so we'd better keep a foot in both camps. Sidle up to the Saudis, get your president to carry a Bible to church, and make sure that CNN is on their toes to catch it. That's just good politics with *the nations* for starters—love your Arab neighbors for sure. And of course, every once in a while, tell God "sorry."

Now I'll tell you sorry; it won't work! The sub-title of our book is *The Rise and Fall of America* and we're beginning to collect some "linguistic" snapshots of performance from page to page!

On my website under *"Israel and the Nations,"* I have a bulletin from September 15, 2007 called, "Who Is America's Best Friend?"[12] Israel would like to think it's them. God-fearing Americans would like to think it's Israel. Both are wrong! If you have to keep watching over your shoulder to make sure that OPEC is not upset, then Israel is *not* your best friend.

Go figure. The Cyruses in today's America may be in church, but hardly in charge. The bottom line is that oil Baals just happen to be the boss. Lord Palmerston proposed the principle for international relations that: "Nations have no permanent friends...they only have permanent interests."

May I suggest that even more of interest is the chummy relationships between the Saudis and all but one of the American presidents across the last four decades—Bible toting or otherwise. Now there are no problems in being friends with foreigners. Maybe they wanted to "witness" to them! Maybe not!

Starting with G.W. Bush's grandfather, Prescott Bush even had a few good friends with the Nazis of grimmer days—grimmer for the Jews at least—while George Bush, Sr. found the Saudis fantastic business partners. No real secrets here. You can Google it all and learn much more than I have time to report. As for nuzzling up with some of the Nazi industrialists, there are several definite references on Answers.com, but nothing of criminality or gross indiscretion has ever been proven, so you can follow it up if you like—probably not worth it.

But look. This is not political witch hunt. I'm not after any president of any political banner. We're after the Baals that throw silver dollars across the Potomac and whether or not we—or anyone—should be searching the shoreline to pick them up! Five of the American Presidents since 1977 have had some "interesting" relationships with the Saudis and their "crude" operations. It's good business if that's your calling—pays well. Who wouldn't if they were in that kind of a business? Except for old King Cyrus—but that's why he remained a king of commitment and not a prince of perversion!

Actually the verses in the Holy Writ about taking bribes are legion. Is there more than one way to absorb a bribe do you suppose?

I have overflowing files over the last decade on such interesting angles as "Saudi Arabia, the 51st State," the Bush Dynasty, Saudi Payola, in addition to tremendous research expertise on many more of these revelations by quality Middle East analysts like Emanuel Winston, Gerald Honigman, Daniel Pipes, and others that would chill your ice cube tray. But again, to tell tales on the tempted and found wanting is *not* my purpose. If God decides that the leaders of the land have not given His Chosen Pilot Project a fair shake, that's His business. And *they* will pay. But I do want to leave you with enough insights that you won't be sent swirling down the neo-Babylonian bubbler crying out, "I wish I had known that"!

The extensive financial interaction that the Bush dynasty maintained with the Saudi Arabian oil interests is beyond belief unless you have been following these mundane matters of mammon with an open mind. Bill Clinton had his more than abundant unadvertised contacts with the Saudis as well. And my, oh my, there was one-time Sunday school teacher Jimmy Carter; I can tell you that his nationalistic interests in the pumping of petrodollars may have been perceptibly crude, yet anything but peanuts!

Of all my bulging files on the Bushes and even office-bound Bill—with both their Saudi friends and their Saudi interests—you would never be able to read even a fraction. Nor could I ever sensibly compress it all into a book. What we have to say here has a far different all over objective than political poppycock, anyway.

Yet, before we close this chapter, we must consider one last excerpt on Jew-judging Jimmy from a report by Jacob Laksin published in *Front Page Magazine* back in December 2006:

"Bluster aside, Carter's chief complaint seems to be that anyone who identifies with Israel, whether in the form of individual support or in a more organized capacity, is incapable of grappling honestly with the issues in the Arab-Israeli conflict. But Carter is poorly placed to make this claim. If such connections alone are sufficient to discredit his critics, then by his own logic Carter is undeserving of a hearing. After all, the Carter Center, the combination research and activist project he founded at Emory University in 1982, has for years prospered from the largesse of assorted Arab financiers.

"Especially lucrative have been Carter's ties to Saudi Arabia. Before his death in 2005, King Fahd was a long-time contributor to the Carter Center and on more than one occasion contributed million-dollar donations. In 1993 alone, the king presented Carter with a gift of $7.6 million. And the king was not the only Saudi royal to commit funds to Carter's cause. As of 2005, the king's high-living nephew, Prince Alwaleed Bin Talal, has donated at least $5 million to the Carter Center." [13]

Sorry, Jimmy, but a verse you may have overlooked from those Sunday school days is:

Do not judge, or you too will be judged; For in the same way you judge others, you will be judged, and with the measure you use, it will be measured to you.[14]

Again, you can Google all of these and much, much more.

Persia in days of old *did* set a precedent of sensitivity to the eternal wisdom of the Almighty, and that from their top man down. It worked. And it blessed the whole nation!

Unfortunately in the USA today, including her financially fixed friends—or better we say *interests*—there's not all that much on the top floor seemingly set to move the Most High! The Cyrus-come-latelies who are made of the kind of spiritual stamina that *might* have blessed the Land of the Free of former times are now all ground floor or even lower!

So let's not get too surprised at some of the toboggan twists and turns on the way down.

[1] Isaiah 44:28; Isaiah 45:1
[2] Compare Matthew 24:9
[3] Romans 11:11-27
[4] I Samuel 15:1-35 Note references to King Agag in verses 20 and 32.
[5] *"Because a hand was against the throne of the Lord"* is an alternate translation of this phrase in the NIV footnote.
[6] Exodus 17:14-16

[7] Matthew 25:40. Also compare Hebrews 13:2 and see Psalms 74:1-20; 137:1-8; Obadiah 1:10; Amos 1:1-15 and a host of parallel Hebrew Scriptures warning of the wrath of God against those who harm His chosen, Jew or Gentile.

[8] Galatians 6:7

[9] Proverbs 29:1 (NKJV) is anathema to the politically correct orientation, but will undoubtedly still be quoted long after the latter have systematically destroyed themselves!

[10] Baal is the generic name in Hebrew of the Canaanite tribal deity, primarily seen as a fertility god including aspects of agriculture and sexuality. Throughout the Hebrew Scriptures, Baal was a constant enticement to the Israelites to idolatry and eventual exile from the Land.

[11] The Riyal is the Saudi Arabian currency.

[12] See "Who Is America's Friend" http://www.spim.org.au/ bulletins/1307.doc

[13] http://www.frontpagemagazine.com/Articles/authors.asp?ID=2454 by Jacob Laksin, Dec 18, 2008.

[14] Matthew 7:1-2

CHAPTER 6

The Glitter That Was Greece

Next we're going to move on to Alexander the Great and his philosopher-forerunners. We might say that Alexander's greatness-title was much of a flipside feature of King Cyrus' greatness. The Greek conqueror's prominence was in military prowess, while Cyrus the Great garnered his title in the considerate way he had traditionally cared for those he had conquered. And history seemed to like that. Obviously the Persian was a tad different than blood-letters before and after him, including sensitivity to his subjects, while according to the records, Alexander was ruthless to say the least.

So now let's have a gander at those Greeks. The Greek-cum-Byzantine culture and influence began more or less in 330 BC when Alexander's advocates cut down the Persian-oriented Darius III to end forever and a day Persia's political dominance of the region.

However, Greece was not just a military superpower per se that lasted a couple of centuries, but a super-influence on world thinking—in particular Western thought—for nearly two millennia. And that latter feature is exactly what we're after in reviewing *the nations* one by one, to perceptively pick up on how God views them.

The stage for Alexander's martial might, however, was set by elite thought peddlers like Socrates, Plato, and Aristotle. These were known as the "big three," but I dealt with them thoroughly enough in my previous book, *Who Told You that You were Naked?* specifically in Chapter 3: *"The Mind Benders Bend Bedrock."* But since what I said there connects like a freight train heading downhill, there is no need to review it here, except to suggest to any and all new readers on the block to check it out.[1] It is, in fact, sort of an overview of what that book is all about. Greek thinking is a prime thread throughout the tapestry of my message.

So not needing to note the military muscle of Alexander for our insights, and having previously pondered the influence of Aristotle and friends on the minds of the Western masses today, we must move on to Pericles. He was number four in influence after the big three, we might say, and both a super statesman and a legend of Athens in his own right. Pericles was born 66 years before Plato and 111 years before Aristotle and was unquestionably an immense influence on both. He was far more a statesman and political figure than either of his two followers. Their primary features were philosophy, not to mention getting rid of God, and then absurdly trying to discover whatever else might be detected in that residual dust of decency!

Both the Delights and Doom of Democracy

Pericles can well be termed as the Daddy of Democracy and, as we begin to think it through, even a blind man with a brain can see the dark hole where democracy is heading these days. Historically, no truly functioning democracy has lasted much over 200 years. As of 2009, America is 233 years old and counting!

Certainly, to appreciate what democracy has given many of the Western nations in the last couple of centuries, one only need to look to tyrannies like the current Zimbabwe, Saudi Arabia, Sudan, and the Darfur massacres. The best these dens of demise can offer is free room and board. Unfortunately, the rooms have bars on the windows, and the board is to sleep on because there is no food! Saudi Arabia is only marginally better. They'll confiscate your

Bible to burn it at the point of entry to "protect" you from their perceptive police who—if *they* found it—would lock you up for life or even worse!

Moreover, I have appreciated living for nearly eight decades in not a few countries where the decent, the dedicated, and the defenseless are protected by honest democratically elected authorities, but that "democratic" bottom is now dropping out like a trapdoor in free fall into a politically corrupt pit of anarchy. Or hadn't you noticed?

Founder and prime proponent of Communism, Karl Marx, countered that his rival economic ideology—capitalism—contains the seeds of its own destruction. In other words, if left to its logical fruition, capitalism will eventually destroy itself. Now if it's disgustingly disloyal to learn anything from an immoral Commie like Karl Marx, you might skip a few paragraphs and go on. On the other hand, we might learn something that even Marx didn't match up with, so let's hang in there and investigate like the Bereans in Acts 17:11.[2] They began to not only search the Scriptures, but to even *think* a tad as they did it! If you're not familiar with the Berean precedent, you can also check them out in Acts 17.[3]

But back to Marx and the seeds of self-destruction, with the awareness that a system that seemingly *begins* brilliantly may even eventually destroy itself. It is therefore ironic that Marx's political passion of Communism went down the drain before capitalism. Already some 60 years ago I read Arthur Koestler's classic published back in 1949: *The God that Failed*. Koestler wrote about the deficiencies of Communism and its inevitable and ultimate collapse.

And collapse it did! In 1989 much like Humpty Dumpty, the Berlin Wall came tumbling down, and with egg on their collective faces, Soviet Communism along with it.

However, now in our own turbulent times, that insight of "seeds of its own destruction" needs be extended from Marx's despised capitalism to democracy in general and liberal democracy in particular. I have long observed that as democracy slides more and more to the left, the logical and inevitable finality of democracy is *anarchy*—no more and no less! It can be no other way.

And all the while, questioning our declining social trends and whitewashed perversion has become such a politically incorrect no-no, that it has long buried any principled boundaries worth fighting for. How do you fight a global thought-tsunami?

In the interim, the lascivious left is ripping to shreds any last semblance of biblical morality. Meanwhile, the phony freedom of anarchy offers a god that neither maintains the integrity one would expect from a sovereign, nor does it wield any power to effect the justice due the little fellow to whom fairness is so facetiously promised. As a tide of mindless anarchy is arising on the one hand, a "democratically" protected Islamic thrust—maneuvering for anni-hilation of the infidel—reaches out on the other. The once caring and protective democracy of yesteryear is disappearing like the morning dew!

Thus it should hardly come as a surprise that likewise, hidden within the Western world's own economic "god of prosperity" are those malignant seeds of anarchy. Democracy becomes usefully en-trapped as the cultural "god of choice," leading down no other garden path but to Political Correctness and that ever-looming One-World government of a New World Order!

See you soon, Nimrod. Hey! Does Babylon ring a bell? We're on our way, Nebbie!

The Failed Fantasy of Banning the Brain

We have an ingeniously catchy non-smoking slogan in Australia found posted in bus stops, public notice boards, and all manner of shopping mall information: "Nobody smokes around here anymore." I'd like to modify that one and spread it across America and the whole of the Western world, "Nobody *thinks* around here anymore!" Come on you Bereans! Where are you?

We can thank Mr. Pericles for some positive insights on how to settle sensitivities among the citizens, but it can *only* work when it does not involve red lines on our bedrock values and morality—that is, God-given biblical values and morality! The Jihadist janitors of history know this full well as they "democratically" sweep up the dust from their terrorism in the wake of ushering in their ultimate aim of a final Caliphate. Yet a mind-boggled West benignly votes on!

Yes, thank you, Mr. Pericles, but no thanks. Your democratic ideas are good enough for city hall perhaps, but it's hardly the God-stuff that we can count on for crunch-time.

Unfortunately, the one-time glory that was Greece turned into one-off glitter, and suddenly it's gone. May we look instead for a kingdom that cannot be shaken!

> *Therefore, since we are receiving a kingdom that cannot be shaken, let us be thankful, and so worship God acceptably with reverence and awe.*[4]

But mere looking may be selling the concept of kingdom living far too short. Nor may we ever confuse kingdom living with kingdom *presuming*, kingdom *preaching* or kingdom *posturing*. Living victoriously while in times of white-water anarchy is made up of a bit stronger stuff!

> *I have told you these things, so that in me you may have peace. In this world you will have trouble. But take heart! I have overcome the world.*[5]

Juggling the pros and cons of even the democracy that once was brings us back to Winston Churchill's colossal conclusion: "Democracy is the worst form of government there is—except for any other."

If I understand Sir Winston right, all human government is a mite complicated—not the least a system that pretends that every last person has the right to have his finger on the panic button—

but such of course is the complexity of the covetousness of human nature. I demand my rights! And added to that, the greater confusion is perhaps the naive human assumption that someone, somewhere—other than the real God, of course—has to run the show from down below.

This naiveté is one-eyed on two counts. The first is the presumption that the human spirit is quite able to govern itself without any hiccups. Of a certainty, the proposition of human government *is* from God. The Almighty says to a floundering flock, "Go ahead and try it and see how you can manage until I eventually show up to check you out." That's the underlying Messianic concept of the Hebrew Scriptures from start to finish. But as we have seen from the kingdoms we have peeked at thus far, not all of the big boys have done all that brilliantly!

But the second blind spot is to naively assume that your particular nation with its particular form of governance is the most celestial system that the human mind could ever contrive! This is a pitfall for every superpower from Nineveh on, as we might note. And worst of all—if it really turns out to be that good—pitfall number two is the human tendency to worship that system, aka idolatry. Sadly, it's been done before. Just check out any ancient Caesar—or even any currently over-booked politician—not to mention his self-satisfied citizens. It just happens!

So guess what! By 2009 Western democracy is now joining anti-capitalist Karl Marx and his Commies as one more failed fantasy in the queue of political ventures that had hoped to ultimately upstage the Ancient of Days for global control. Even though the democratic experiment has lasted for a mite more than the statistical probability of two centuries, it's a cold comfort that it *did* outlast poor caved-in Karl on the Soviet stage. The only way a greedy liberal democracy has been working anyway in her dying days was to hire a laser sharp team of lawyers to slice up a personal piece of pie in the sky. The bad news is that 98% of the populace can't afford even one lawyer let alone a team, and the downturn is doing the rest!

You came up with some good ideas, Mr. Pericles, but it looks like she ain't gonna fly very high anymore! Wait till the freedom-worshippers of former times find that one out! They had swallowed democratic freedoms like the big fish fed on Jonah!

Even more serious than those mind-boggled voters we mentioned a few lines above, is a mind-boggled church that has merged its god with a political system and idolatrously worships on!

So much for the presumed democratic designer-god heading into a New World Order! The greatest thing since sliced bread has now become burned toast!

At the moment, I'm at a bus stop waiting for the next bus marked Isaiah 64:1: *"Oh, that you would rend the heavens and come down, that the mountains would tremble before you!"*

Peeking Within Pericles' Personal Portfolio

And if you're really ready for your next tummy ache, you ought to read Answers.com's biography on Pericles. They have several bio's on him, but the first one is the most complete, and without question, the easiest one to find.

Mr. P shockingly had a dog-eat-dog democratic lifestyle of a not so merry merry-go-round of chasing your enemy's tail while watching out for your own. He democratically bantered with round-robin assassination advocates like his most dangerous colleague-cum-adversary—or was it just the reverse—named General Cimon. But additional assassins of the Areopagas kept life even more interesting and death even closer. And there were added sparring partners from Sparta, peril with Persia, catastrophe from Corfu, avoiding eradication by Egypt, backstabbing from Samos—you name it! Just thought you might like to know where our cherished democracy actually hailed from. No wonder they exported it to the West!

Quoting from the Answers.com biography:

> "To admirers of Democracy, he (Pericles) is almost without a peer. The society which he led was imbued with his ideas—an overmastering love of Athens (aka worshipping of a nation), a passionate belief in freedom (for which the Bible has its own definition) for Athenians and of faith in the ability of man (i.e. humanism)."

The parenthetical notations are mine to make it easier to pick up the bottom line. "Help Wanted: God need not apply."

So in winding down with our democracy-bestowing Athenian statesman, Pericles, may I note that Hellenistic humanism (aka democracy) is not the only legacy that the clever thinking ancients blessed us with, to replace the "bondage" of our Bibles with freedom-cum-anarchy. It did take some time—like a couple of centuries.

Wait a minute! Do I hear someone out there fussing that this is just one more rambling political tirade? Not quite! Not unless the King of the Universe is one more cheap politician and the Bible is His constitution!

Democracy Is the End Game of Godless Guesswork

Certainly, we have thus far been looking at much of what has happened politically across the millennia, and in fact still is happening today on the ground. These are basic insights of the facts of life.

But the most significant wrap-up of this whole matter is, first of all, some interesting linguistic insights which could be a bit eye opening, while the bottom line takes us straight back to the Scripture to put it all together.

Let's do a bit of word study to clarify our thinking. What is the *opposite* of democracy? Communism? That's not even close unless one is limited to comparing economic systems, but I'd like to revert to basic word meanings. What about tyranny? That's not very close either. I've got a good friend—a bit of a Berean type—who reckons that democracy is the tyranny of the 51% over 49%. He's got a point. Maybe that's what Churchill was thinking about?

Let's take it from the other end. What are the basic synonyms for democracy? Free choice? Not bad. Self will? Getting very close! In fact it's also getting very close to Genesis 3:3-5:

> *...but God did say, "You must not eat fruit from the tree that is in the middle of the garden, and you must not touch it, or you will die." "You will not surely die," the serpent said to the woman. "For God knows that when you eat of it your eyes will be opened, and you will be like God, knowing good and evil."*

Taking the option of nibbling on the original forbidden fruit when told not to is light-years beyond and apart from mere disobedience. Disobedience is a generic term with a broad range of meaning. It could be good; it could be bad, depending on the circumstances. It could be fixed quite easily with a U-turn. Or it may be far more difficult to adjust. It could be an act; it could be an attitude.

The Garden scenario of Genesis 3, on the other hand, unveils the entire biblical divide of the Almighty's relationship with His human creation, and His human creature's relationship to Him. Genesis 3 is humanity's first step into the watershed of history.[6] The significance of this particular Tree of Forbidden Fruit therefore has a far-reaching impact *beyond* just "breaking the rules." Rather it is overtly maintaining that we are wise enough to make our own choices, so move over anyone else whoever you may be! And that obviously includes the King of Creation.

Unfortunately the Hellenist-based Periclean mindset is perched perilously on that brink. And as the globe shrinks and the world withers to end-of-days proportions, the designer cult of a New World Order showdown is built upon self will. *Indeed we can!*

I'm sorry! Who can? Calling all thinking Bereans! We've got a "can" problem.

Over the eons of time, a national leader is usually someone who has been around the block for a few times, even if his (or her) selection is by birth, by battle, by tyranny, or even more recently by ballot box. Unfortunately, there have been bad apples in every barrel of bygone days. Plenty!

But in this overview, I'm not so much interested in what "they" did, and certainly not what "they" are saying now, but what the Good Book has recorded for us. There has been an interesting track record of failure when the leader or leaders responded to what the people wanted. Just to cite a few:

• Aaron listened to the people and created the golden calf in Exodus 32:22-23.

• Ten of the twelve spies who checked out Canaan won the vote but disastrously lost their lives in the desert, as well as a 40-year slog in the boonies for everyone else in Deuteronomy 1:19-36.

• Korah and a significant contingent of the community opted to oust Moses for new leadership, and the earth opened and swallowed them whole in Numbers 16.

• King Saul "feared the people" in 1 Samuel 15:24-26 and lost his kingdom to David.

• In Acts 27:9-26 the centurion listened to the ship's captain and crew instead of to Paul and lost his entire ship and nearly 276 lives as well.

And the biblical examples go on and on. The Scriptures are replete with a focus on the fact that one plus God is a majority, and never mind the masses!

There are, of course, human reasons to take into consideration such as age, experience, or the mindset of the monarch versus his multitudes. Bribery, corruption and ingenious counting[7] add to the mix. But even beyond that, the track record of the persuasion of the people in the Bible is less than impressive! The Scriptures on the other hand are the record of a sovereign voice, and hardly the hangers-on of humanism.

May the Western worshippers of the ballot box finally get it into their heads that their forms of government are not bad—certainly better than some—but have hardly been hatched from the Holy Writ.

Therefore, so much for politics, politicians, deceptive dealings, and democratic downturns! What yesterday's democracy now faces in the future is anyone's guess. In fact from 2009 on is monumental guesswork. Fasten your seatbelts!

Aristotle Upstages the Almighty—but Only for the Moment

Therefore, finally, let us close with Aristotle, the last-in-line of the Hellenist philosophers. He was the one who really tied the beautiful bow on that priceless gift package of "God-riddance."

May we ponder again for a few Berean-modeled moments what all Aristotle's rejection of any metaphysical dimension—good spirits or bad—had actually effected. From the Almighty to the demonic—with one Aristotelian broom—it was a clean sweep, leaving nothing more than man, man, and more man to make the decisions!

Moreover his thinking has by now saturated the entire Western world, and not the least a religious church that professes one thing and yet unwittingly believes quite another. After all if all the world presumably assumes there is neither good nor evil, neither a God nor even a devil, the candor becomes a bit infectious. So if for old time's sake we "play" church, try to be nice most of the time, and possibly even keep a memo of the Creator around our necks— maybe a cross—we're practically home free!

Just muse a bit more, Berean friends. May we take a few less than clever clues from that hate-riddled hierarchy of "God-helpers" some 2000 years ago in Jerusalem who put the Most High on hold just long enough to settle a more personal score of jealousy! In unadulterated hypocrisy: *"We have no King but Caesar."*[8]

But before pointing any fingers of prejudice, do you know any "good Gentile Christians" nowadays who blatantly use the identical rationale? They are astute enough not to actually put it into words, but in their heart of hearts they shout it from the housetops: "We have no dominion over us but democracy."

So guess who finally looked the other way to let the Religious Right get clobbered in the November 2008 elections? It looks like democracy really has not been the best Abba after all!

This is not exactly a good time to say, "Amen." It's a good time to wake up and start saying sorry to the real God!

---

[1] Victor Schlatter, *Who Told You That You Were Naked?*, (Shippensburg, PA: Destiny Image Publishers, 2006). Chapter , "The *Mind Benders Bend Bedrock.*"

[2] *"Now the Bereans were of more noble character than the Thessalonians, for they received the message with great eagerness and examined the Scriptures every day to see if what Paul said was true."*

[3] See Acts 17:10,11 and 14; 20:4

[4] Hebrews 12:28

[5] John 16:33.

[6] See Victor Schlatter above. Again, much of this is covered in *Who Told You that You Were Naked?* (Shippensburg, PA: Destiny Image Publishers, 2006).

[7] It has been reported that it was Josef Stalin who said: "It doesn't matter who votes; it matters only who counts the votes."

[8] John 19:15b

CHAPTER 7

Caesar Ain't Gonna Like This!

Before we go any further, let's just make sure we're on the same page and *not* heading north toward places like Mount Saphon where they used to bow to Baal. We frown on that these days!

We started out by noting that *the nations* as understood in the Good Book were not always found in favor of the Most High, and the reason for that was most probably because they weren't all that impressed with His snooping around in their personal international affairs either. It was—and still is—a less than chummy standoff we might say.

Abba created them all, but in those early days, *the nations* didn't have a diplomat on duty checking out the creation to verify whether or not it actually happened according to tradition. So there was a bit of a stalemate until Charlie Darwin came along and told them not to worry too much about it. From then on there was an even greater rift in the relationship, and so it goes!

Let's face it; the Creator favors accountability, while the created mortals frequently do not like to be accountable to anyone, so we've got a problem.

Moreover, I think that it's important to note that both the scriptural account of *the nations* together with secular records from archaeology revealed enough reinforcement that we could accept a sense of accuracy. Someone *is* out there!

The World Stage

So if "All the world's a stage," as William Shakespeare so superbly suggested, the Ninevites came on first but were so fiercely fighting friends and neighbors with such passion, they scarcely noticed whether the Almighty was actually interested in their gruesome pastimes or not.

The Babylonians who followed them boasted that regardless of whether or not the Creator was still in business, their gods from under every green tree were just as capable—if not better—than anything from bygone Garden grottos.

A more astute Persian Cyrus did presume a preferable God might actually be found in Jerusalem and certainly did profit from that insight. But when the Greek thinkers came along next, they blew it with any knowledgeable notes from History 101. A secular-anchored Aristotle mindlessly taught that anything of a spiritual dimension was merely of the mind and woefully widened the distance from an earthbound fall into the darkness on up to heaven's Creator of light.

But next came the Roman Empire. Though many of Rome's teachers virtually worshipped the Hellenist Aristotle (the human brain behind the casting off of anything celestial), some of her more astute souls may have suspected that those secular mockers of a spirit-world had perhaps gone too far.

After all the wild blue yonder has always yearned for gods of some sort; so let's collectively be a god ourselves, the Romans reflected! Thus from those brutal and coldblooded Caesars to an eventually more soberly-cast Constantine—from the secular to the sedate—they began to polish their haloes.

The Caesars Play God

So let's play God! Who said Roman gods had to be compassionate? So the Caesars began to roll on to the stage from left, right, and center roaring, "Fair enough, but if we're going to be gods we're going to be gods, and we're going to be tough!" So from here on out, if we hear that there's any other claim to be the Lord of the land, he's in trouble with us. We've got hungry lions to be fed and heaps of front row seats left for sale at the circus!

The Caesars and Emperors who followed them ruled with a heavy hand from Augustus in 27 BC through the reign of Emperor Marcus Aurelius that ended in 180 AD—the 200 years of Pax Romana—the "Peace of Rome." Those citizens who were nominally pagan and bowed before the emperors fared fairly well in those days, but to the God-fearing believers—Christian or Jewish—it was a far different tale of woe proceeding to the pain of torture and death. Peace, peace, but there was no peace for any admirers of the Most High!

And so it was. But may we now move on to contemplate the two tiers of deity of the Roman Empire that in one form or another spanned some 500 years of both martial as well as cultural influence. And all that time the Ancient of Days looked on and, I would suspect, even took a few notes!

Moreover, we find in the Scriptures that when asked if one should pay taxes to these ruthless rogues, Abba's Right-hand Man returned comments like:

If all those mercenaries want is money, give it to them; My Kingdom is not of this world and has a far different value system, but they wouldn't understand that.[1]

Or on another occasion He said:

I tell you, my friends, do not be afraid of those who kill the body and after that can do no more. But I will show you whom you should fear: Fear him who, after the killing of the body, has power to throw you into hell. Yes, I tell you, fear him.[2]

Militarily with the Caesars, Rome got off the ground as a flint-steel super force. Since Rome was a potent political entity, no one dared question her sovereignty—neither Jew, nor Gentile, nor heretic cult. But was this an ironic accident or a well-planned twitch of fate?

A King the Caesars Hadn't Counted On

Someone else a bit higher also had an eye on global destiny at almost the same time that the Caesars got going, selecting that very era of Pax Romana to pull it off. In 27 BC, Augustus Caesar had come on stage and started stirring the pot of international stew. Some twenty three years later depending on who's minding the calendar months, a tiny little Jewish bundle was born in Bethlehem.[3]

Life in and around Jerusalem and Bethlehem had been much on the back-burner in those days. Some were still chaffing at losing their own global supremacy, aka Solomon's Golden Years, some five centuries earlier. Thus, the Jews in the aftermath of intermittent bashings from Greek hegemony, sacred temple desecrations, and less than sanctified syncretism with Hellenist mind-benders—at an obscure moment when the masses happened to be looking else-where—the new little babe slipped in by the back door in the city of David. Few noticed the event. Most assumed that she was merely an unwed mama banished to the barn, and since the Angel Show didn't come on stage until way after midnight, only a minute handful of locals managed to show up!

Ironically King Herod, Emperor Augustus's Jerusalem-based hit man, caught word of it, and to make sure his rumored replace-ment didn't ever see the light of day, he had all the tiny tykes of the town massacred. Indeed it was a bit grim, but this was neither the first nor the last time that Herod the Gross did such things. He even murdered his wife and not a few other close relatives over var-ious incidental issues! Moreover, up to this very day, such horrible things periodically happen to Jewish children in a grossly anti-Semitic world!

You know the story. Herod's underlings missed one, and this

indeed was the One who grew up to counter-balance the malevo-lence of Rome. But it was hardly restricted to Rome's rebellious-ness. It rewrote a proposed balance sheet for all *the nations*, including superpowers from that day forward—and even retroac-tively reached all the way back to Babylon!

Something You Could Count On

But there is another incredible thing that happened involving that exact era. Though most of the nations gave neither hoot nor whistle for the young lad, he grew up to be labeled by a semi-sar-castic, yet semi-nervous Governor Pilate as "the King of the Jews."[4] Can you believe that even though masses throughout the Orient and the Southern Hemisphere were not tuned in those days, the gamut of the Western globe—after a few centuries to think it over—began realigning not their sundials, but their calendars to this specific timeframe of history!

The post-Caesar Romans (bless their pointed little spears) began calling the days as Anno Domini, that is: "In the year of our Lord" and BC, that is: "Before Christ." If the arrival of this little fellow who was and still is treated as so blasé by billions of by-standers, who is making this happen? For that matter, for those of other persuasions who have not been all that impressed with the advent of the *King of the Jews,* an alternative CE—for Common Era—is used to replace AD, and BCE—Before the Common Era—substitutes for BC. But could anyone please explain why even the "Common Era" of a largely godless globe, came to signify the advent that it does?

Was this a part of the script of the players *on* the stage, or was it a sly wink from the One who *owns* the stage?

Battling for the Brain aka Political Correctness

Regardless, let's now back up for an overview of this midpoint era of Rome's rather lengthy day under the sun. Lengthy indeed, but something quite new was taking place on center stage.

After some four millennia of international conquerors (aka superpowers) from Nimrod's Nineveh on to Alexander's Greece, they all had done battle by blade and blood, but Alexander's preceding philosophers shoehorned an entirely new finesse in fighting. The thought-provoking Hellenists introduced a novel element of psychological reinvention of reality—the battle for the mind!

Rome was perhaps the first to implement this innovation, but hardly the last. Have you ever heard of media propaganda? Have you ever deeply pondered the root—not roots—of Political Correctness?[5] Keep this on file for the final chapters of this book, but nuclear nightmare without the nearly impenetrable backup of global media propaganda is a non-starter. And this of course includes an Islamic reinvention of medieval history, as well as those poster parading one-liners from thought-merchants of a politically correct One World Government!

Woe to those who call evil good and good evil, who put darkness for light and light for darkness, who put bitter for sweet and sweet for bitter.[6]

Let's take one more step back and review this very seriously. The Caesars in Jesus' day—I personally like to call Him Yeshua—totally coveted the top perch and were grossly offended at this God-of-heaven thing touted by true believers. Thus they needed no written permission to stamp out any and all insubordination from Jew, Gentile, or anything in between that didn't call Caesar Lord, a title—unfortunately for them—that the Most High had reserved for Himself since Genesis 1:1: *"In the beginning God..."*

Of course, the sons of Abraham were already on side with who was *really* Lord. Moreover there were Gentiles from *the nations* who also wanted to come to the party at the invitation of Yeshua, and also recognized the Almighty as Lord as any good Jew was wont to do. Sadly both sides of the family became instant persona non grata to the Caesars who didn't know Abba from Adam, nor did they care. Nor did they cherish any rivalry with who may be the real Power on the planet!

So under their craze to crush any and all competition with their own presumed god-status, the rulers of Rome took on both the Jew bound to his heritage or Gentile who dared consider the concept of a Jewish Messiah. Sadly they frequently used other Jews to savage those degenerate "blasphemers" for their flawed messianic concept of heaven-sent help. Thus to repress the mushrooming masses of Gentile believers—many of whom due to the Assyrian dispersion of 724 BC may well have held a few long-lost Hebraic genes as well—were either fed to the lions or bled by the sword. Any heresy against a god-like Caesar was remedied only by execution. Nevertheless, with either committed Jew or believing Gentile dedicated to the God of the galaxies, the roots of their faith delved far more deeply than any pain of death and torture.

The rest of the story is history—though many Jews and Gentiles were a bit hard put to accurately assess what was really happening and why, since both groups were also harshly cast into enmity with one another. The Caesars deviously played both ends against the middle and brutally butchered both Jew *and* Gentile believers who recognized that the Abba of Abraham and the Abba of Yeshua was the one and the same Creator of the Universe—actually *King of the Universe* in all Jewish prayers.

Constantine's Crafty Curriculum

But times were a changin'. And this facet of thinking-driven bloodletters first surfaced almost 1700 years ago with Rome's "gettin' religion" for the final phase of the Empire.

The old guard of kill and overcome never ceased to flow freely on in the political side of the Caesars. But eventually the psychological side of the purpose driven conquerors surfaced in 325 AD when Constantine figured that if you can't beat 'em, join 'em. So Emperor Connie, with wine and wafer in hand, took over the church!

And as the numbers of non-Jewish believers in a Jewish God grew beyond proportion in 325 AD, Emperor Constantine the Great took the gamble. He fled with the faithful.

Well, not exactly. He fled nowhere! Rather he took charge of the "church." Up until then, from time to time the former Caesars did have their little helpers to divide and conquer whatever affinity did remain between new Gentile believers and a less-than-impressed Jewish hierarchy. But Constantine's capitulation altered everything from semi-ragged relationships to out and out anti-Semitism. Those former goal posts had been ingeniously moved to a newly conned footing!

But let us not call *all* those Gentiles "Christians" just yet because this label has a few side trails of semantics if not commitment. Moreover, these levels of understanding of what a Christian actually is did *not* become a full-blown hiccup until *after* Constantine stepped in. I do *not* say that there were no theological misunderstandings before Con and Company shifted those goal posts in the direction of the Greek polytheists, even though counting how many gods the Church actually worshipped soon *did* become a problem!

I won't further elaborate on this at the moment except that my Bible hints that Abba may have a grand plan of His own to bring all the believing family of one and only one God around the *erev* Shabbat table[7] at least by the end of days. There is still a tad of time left to probe a few of the possibilities. But for those of us who watch the walls of Jerusalem,[8] however the Most High decides to do it will quite probably get the approval of the rest of us, except for a few die-hard Replacement Theologians for whom reality may take a day or so longer to digest!

But of course, we'd hardly expect any of the emperor-types

would show up for any such non-Caesar bash—then or now! It will be interesting to watch which will be the first—the politicians or the Replacement preachers—to be able to modify their mindsets should the judgments handed down from the Top come a tad differently than what they had supposed!

Ironically, a little more than a century before Constantine's U-turn, Gentile believers had been bitterly persecuted by Emperor Marcus Aurelius,[9] but by early in the fourth century AD this new concept of Christianity became legitimately wedded to the state and persecution of Gentiles within the newly recognized Church ceased. Sadly the world's oldest scapegoat—the Jew—did not fare quite so well. Finding themselves the not-so-kosher meat in the sandwich, anti-Semitism languished on.

And with the help of a Hellenistic precedent for maneuvering the mind, Rome became the first superpower—or super-culture if you please—to face two well-defined fronts of conquest or defense. War therefore remained as a conqueror of new domain along with defense of past conquests on one hand, or it alternatively became a launching pad to propagate new ideology or to defend political beliefs and principles on the other.

And as for Constantine—giving him the benefit of the doubt for his motives—he nevertheless grossly missed the mark in redefining the Ancient of Days and rewriting the script. Europe as well grossly missed the mark as we shall pursue in the following chapter. America polished her halo and shined her Sunday-go-to-meetin' shoes as well. This is not to say there were not a lot of good caring people from Connie to the California Gold rush as it were, but to remind us that in the eye of the King of Creation, all *the nations* have always been just a little bit naughty! Let's never forget: *"All have sinned and fall short of the glory of God."*[10]

Today a perverse world is stuck with an evolving godless, prejudiced, and morally bankrupt United Nations, whose hapless, global citizens find themselves a long, long way from home!

Is War from Satan or from Men?

Moreover, now in nearly 2000 years of a gradually ascending two-front mentality, the United Nations and the peace mongers are decrying the original option of bloodshed—and who would not agree with a peace-making principle? But for nations in general and Israel in particular, peacemaking is *not* war "denial" but war winning. It's not hiding in a hole until Lucifer repents but responding strongly until Lucifer gets lost!

Question: Is war satanic? If it isn't, the alternative must be for everyone to join in the fun and games—like the Politically Correct anarchy that is rising like a life-suffocating tsunami in every quarter![11] But if war *is* satanic, then under the auspices of the Almighty, it must be won!

The memorable quote most often attributed to Edmund Burke speaks volumes to the fearful: "All that is necessary for evil to triumph is for good men to do nothing."

So are we in a battle or is life merely throwing the dice in a grand game of Monopoly? Having seen His Majesty in a scientifically ordered universe, His wisdom in my Bible and His linkage in my relationships with both Him and His Family, I can't buy the second option!

But the treachery is that in the current undermining of the morals of men by peaceful protest coupled with a physically less-than-visible God is a much softer target, and far harder to counter. Reinforced by the "new morality" of the 1960s, we are now approaching 70 years of pseudo-peace since the end of WWII, a peace that is fueled by manipulated media propaganda. It serves to whitewash the old immorality with a tidal wave of Political Correctness that inundates standards of human decency laid out from time immemorial in bedrock Scripture. Needless to say, peace is farther off than ever!

Gideon, His God, and the Road Least Regarded

Before we finish these concerns—and by the way, "Caesar ain't gonna like this one"—there's a classic reflection of where we are currently at in the story of Gideon in Chapter 6 of the book of Judges. Better we read some of it:

> *Again the Israelites did evil in the eyes of the LORD, and for seven years he gave them into the hands of the Midianites. Because the power of Midian was so oppressive, the Israelites prepared **shelters for themselves in mountain clefts, caves and strongholds**. Whenever the Israelites planted their crops, the Midianites, Amalekites and other eastern peoples invaded the country. They camped on the land and ruined the crops all the way to Gaza and did not spare a living thing for Israel, neither sheep nor cattle nor donkeys. They came up with their livestock and their tents like swarms of locusts. It was impossible to count the men and their camels; they invaded the land to ravage it. Midian so impoverished the Israelites that they cried out to the LORD for help* (emphasis added).[12]

And the saga continues:

> *When the Israelites cried to the LORD because of Midian, he sent them a prophet, who said, "This is what the LORD, the God of Israel, says: I brought you up out of Egypt, out of the land of slavery. I snatched you from the power of Egypt and from the hand of all your oppressors. I drove them from before you and gave you their land. I said to you, I am the LORD your God; do not worship the gods of the Amorites, in whose land you live." But you have not listened to me.*[13]

To make a long story short, God then found young Gideon hiding in a winepress shaking like a grape leaf and challenged him to go after the Midianites camped in the Jezreel Valley (which by the way is a stone's throw from Armageddon).

I've been through that area over a dozen times myself. That entire valley full of Midianites, Amalekites, and allies stretched from the base of Mt. Moreh to the north all the way to the foot of Mt. Gilboa on the south would be quite sobering a spectacle I might say.

The Midianites, the Amalekites and all the other eastern peoples had settled in the valley, thick as locusts. Their camels could no more be counted than the sand on the seashore. [14]

So in the darkness young Gideon and his 300 Israelite companions stealthily surrounded that massive camp at widely spaced intervals. Knowing the area, I can just visualize this massive miracle!

Then at Gideon's midnight trumpet blast they all simultaneously flashed their torches and blew their shofars in unison and scared the socks—sandals I should say—off the raiders who cleared out of there somewhere in the direction of Saudi Sands Retreat Grounds like Katusha rockets in overdrive!

And guess what—you can pass this on to the United Nations if you like—Gideon himself didn't shed one drop of blood. But don't tell the UN that the Jews won the battle, or they'll have them in the dock for something—maybe disproportionate force! That's Abba, and He is the same, yesterday, today, and forever!

So this is anything but to advocate bloodshed. But what the world in general, and the UN in particular, needs to understand is that war from the ancients on, was never allowed for weasels to hide underground; war was allowed by the Almighty to win—Gideon style!

But may I let you in on a little secret that the United Nations and their Heinz 57 handlers[15] have either naively overlooked, or are trying to not-so-cunningly conceal in order to placate their 57 prime promoters. No more war! No more war! No more war! Indeed, it would be wonderful!

But thanks to non-thinkers of the globe, victims in Dafur, Afghanistan, Iraq, Israel—both Jews and Arabs—are dying like flies, because when a war is won there is peace—real peace, at least for an appreciable time.

Yet, the Almighty has allowed the bloodshed of war for two reasons: Either it is a judgment on the guilty to be punished—the rain falling on the just or on the unjust—or contrariwise, a non-responsive "heaven of brass" that is slow to reply to the cries of the offended because of a long-term need of someone, somewhere to get it right with Him. If you can find any other reason in the Good Book for the outcome of wars, let me know.

If Abba has gone on holidays—or even gone for good—you can cheer the UN for their splendid stand in. If not, it's what we have suspected all along!

When war is stopped inconclusively for deceitful designs such as "disproportionate force," one-sided "war crimes," or conniving treaties to allow terrorists to amass a few more thousand missiles—the bloodletting flows on, and on, and on.

I'm sure we all have more than a hunch that Lucifer's lads are behind all war anyway, but to give the ever-fumbling United Nations and friends the benefit of the doubt, perhaps they are a just a bit slow of intellect and not the slightest bit conniving! But the moment of truth is that the peace mongers are the very ones who are prolonging the pain and upping the bloodbaths around the globe.

Our purpose across these pages is neither to praise Rome's political prowess and military power in the halls of history, nor is it—as many have done and yet wish to do—in judging her moral manipulations over the centuries. I'm sure the Almighty will be quite capable of sorting His notes, crowns, and charge sheets. After all, the stage is Abba's to mount for the last curtain call. He was the one who chose Rome to be holding the reins at both the juncture of psychological warfare as well as the advent of His Messiah.

And who knew war better than Rome? But unfortunately what the Caesars never did figure out was the Ancient of Days' eternal mystery of war and peace. From the birth of a baby[16] to bloodshed of *the nations*[17] to the atonement of the sinner[18]—without the pain, you'll never know the peace! And what else is new? Modern propaganda and plenty of it!

1 My very casual paraphrase from Mark 12:14-17, and again from John 18:36
2 Luke 12:4-5
3 See full story in Luke 2:1-40.
4 John 19:19-21
5 See Victor Schlatter, *Who Told You that You Were Naked?* (Shippensburg, PA: Destiny Image, 2006), Chapter 11: *With Political Correctness Who Needs an Antichrist?*
6 Isaiah 5:20
7 *Erev* is Hebrew for *evening* and *erev Shabbat* is the Jewish family meal carefully kept every Friday evening by religious Jews as well as most Messianic Jews or even some Gentiles who believe that Yeshua was actually the first appearance of the Messiah.
8 See Isaiah 62:6-7
9 See http://www.answers.com/topic/marcus-aurelius; Scroll down to *Who2Biography* or *Columbia Encyclopedia*.
10 Romans 3:23
11 See Zechariah 8:10, 2 Chronicles 15:5: Judges 21:25.
12 Judges 6:1-6
13 Judges 6:7-10
14 Judges 7:12
15 The reference has nothing to do with the reputable people of Heinz or their fine products, but everything to do with a tongue in cheek reference to the coincidental number of the group of 57 key UN affiliates who maintain a biased policy against Israel and the nations who respect her.
16 John 16:21
17 John 16:33
18 Exodus 24:6-8; Leviticus 17:11; Hebrews 9:18-22.

CHAPTER 8

Constantine's Kids

We perceive from the last chapter that, in the cunning of Rome, Emperor Constantine came to the conclusion that if you can't massacre that multitude of defectors who are fleeing to the Most High—then marry them. So marry them he did! But like many of today's dubious matches, what are the kids going to be like?

With all due regard for a declining count of believers from Britain to Brussels, Europe is that figurative family. So what have the *kinder* of Constantine grown up to be over the centuries? Mind you, I have spent decades in developing areas of the Third World, and people who have lived in grass houses should never stow the thrones of kings and queens of royalty!

But back to all seriousness, I'll try my best to study Abba's balance sheet of values and virtues of Europe versus capital gains or castles in the sky.

The Pros and Cons of Historic Europe

Europe has done some commendable things over the centuries which we cannot deny. For a certainty Con's kids have taken the message of a higher King than Caesar across the globe. My only moment of concern is that there is a vast difference between religion and righteousness. But I'll defer to the Almighty to tap the final gavel on that one. Spreading the message that there is a King a bit above humankind is certainly a great leap forward after the audacity of Aristotle.

The crusades and colonialism had both their pros and cons (pun intended). Let's look at the crusades first: The pros (no pun intended) were Charles Martel who stopped the Spanish Islamic advance at Tours, France, in 734 AD, and one brave Polish Commander, Jan Sobieski and comrades who stopped a major Turkish onslaught at Vienna in 1683.[1] "Christian" Europe at that time—and this is a non-judgment on how deep that Christianity may have penetrated into the heavenlies—needed the anti-God competition then no more than it needs it now!

The cons, nevertheless, produced far more doubtful achievements. Out of eight crusades from 1095 to 1291, one less than brilliant bystander reckoned the crusades were "good for business" (*commerce* he called it), while the real truth was that a lot of European, Arab, and Jewish blood (the latter who were not even involved in the fighting) flowed freely and—much like most mayhem—zero was accomplished other than gross atrocities.[2]

So what about colonialism? Good for business once again—far more for the coffers of Europe we might note, and a much less measured amount for the token takings throughout the far off ports of call. I highly recommend you look up my former findings on the matter in Chapter 10 of my previous book, *Showdown of the Gods*. I called the chapter: "If God Loves Poor Folks, Why Not Make a Few More?"[3] which hints a touch of truth to what we might expect to find!

As I have mentioned in the past, those messengers of the faith often shared a voyage on the same vessels that supplied the homeland with more earthy matters like diamonds, gold, spices, and such. This naturally could cast somewhat of a dubious shadow—unless the sailing was at night when shadows are the norm! Nevertheless, let's give credit where credit is due. If the message was one of relationship with Abba and not mere religious rote with a foreign flavor, we can hardly fault that.

Unfortunately colonialism did have a few other less than favorable features like unmitigated greed which generally catches the lusting eye of most of *the nations*, not to mention their kings. But otherwise, as we might expect, greed has never rated all that high in the Good Book!

But worst of all was the slave trade for which one would be in dire straits to find the tiniest trace of goodness. The fact that the Arabs as well as the Americans were also involved up to their eyeballs in this pitiful practice hardly offers the slightest justification. It only makes it the more merciless.

Yet the Almighty has an amazing capacity to cultivate virtue in a cesspool of corruption, like a lone daffodil struggling for life in a desolate desert. Or the tiny spider that reflects a wisp of life to a prisoner of conscience vegetating in a dungeon of despair! Yet a ray of hope from the darkness of slavery and separation from every facet of home that the cringing captive might once have known was: "Amazing Grace, how sweet the sound that saved a wretch like me...."[4] Sometime slave-master, John Newton's *Amazing Grace* arose like a phoenix from the ashes of the brutality of slavery.

Out of the pit of hell, John Newton, a scurrilous young British sailor was transformed from a profiteer on the sacredness of human life and the crushed souls of black Africans, into an avenger of the evil depths of the slave trade. Young Newton himself eventually became actively involved in the abolition of slave trading in Britain in the late 1880s.

A Closer View of the Virtues

This might be a good time to note a few other honorable highlights arising from oft-gilded and never far from a bread and butter, down to earth, secular, humanistic Europe. My cry in these pages is about a world that needs purpose more than prestige; a brain on the altar more than bread on the table;[5] principles held by the oppressed more than added vitality from Vitamin B; and a God to hear with the ears, much more than gold to hoard with the fist. And I might add that Europe *has* produced some gems that were far greater quality than those coveted diamonds of South Africa!

The first that come to mind were the Wesleys of Britain, John Wycliffe, John Huss. John Knox of Scotland, Ulrich Zwingli, Menno Simons, and a flood of fellow Anabaptists, the Waldenses, the Huguenots, and a few of more recent vintage with the likes of C.S. Lewis, or Francis Schaffer.

The list is long. Forgive me if I have failed to include one of your cherished few though I confess I might have bypassed a couple of the "faithful" who favored firing up any and all of their heretic colleagues—literally! But there were other towers of truth taller than tradition.

The scientists of mercy and those who worked miracles in medicine dare not be overlooked, in particular not a few Jews whose contributions of life saving genius are too many to mention. And there were the additional multitude of servants to humankind whose names are yet obscure. Europe has been richly endowed with memorable legends. But on the other hand, crowns and kudos are supposed to eventually go to the feet of the King of kings anyway.[6]

Hosts of individuals frequently paid with their own blood in resisting through their faith or conscience politically totalitarian or religious regimes. After all, unless you've been mentally hijacked as a Hellenist and re-programmed to think that there is no sovereign authority higher than the human head, giving glory to a Creator God must be the bottom line anyway. It was the Ancient of Days that set this whole human orchestration into motion in the first place—you and I certainly didn't have a hand in the matter!

What's the Price Tag of Anything Less than Virtuous

Indeed, quite a few fancy bouquets of roses came out of a quaint and nostalgic Europe in her day. But can I be honest? Dare

I tell the truth? I'm going to have to tell the truth when we get to the "Good Ole USA" too, and that might even be a tad harder! But no nation will crash those pearly gates without a bit of accountability first. I'm not talking about being "saved." The point is that what your community does, what your society allows, what your nation legislates will forever and a day put the sharp stones in your path and thorns on your bouquets! Just be aware of that.

A friend not long ago reminded me that old age was not for sissies. I'd like to remind us all that *life* is not for sissies. Moreover, I'm advising one and all to keep catching out of the corner of your eye just who happens to be poised at the top of the totem pole! It's not you and it's not me, and it's certainly not our governments. Keep your eye on the only One who counts!

Therefore all bouquets of flashy roses do have a few thorns even if they're from Paris! We're not quite done with that colonial bit yet. Who knows there's a price tag on cutting corners? Taking advantage of a neighbor who trusts you? What about taking advantage of a less-learned client from "those faraway places with the strange sounding names"? Who recalls that greed is that other word for covet in the Ten Commandments?

Oh, no, no! I'm not pointing anyone out personally! This is about corporations—*the nations*; this means a massive insulation between the indirect benefactor and those who are *"done by."* Remember Shakespeare's *Merchant of Venice* and the pound of flesh thing?[7] Guarantor Antonio was supposed to yield up a "pound of flesh closest to his heart" if the debt in question was not paid. And fate determined that it was not!

To get to the point (aka: the thorn on the rose), I have lived long enough in the Third World to know that there is *always* an unwritten price to pay for what the Westerner—blinded by his own ego, his self importance, and indeed his own greed—does not yet see!

But of course this is not to say that Ahmed standing back on the dock in Port Aden might not be a bit slippery either! And among a grand gamut of thousands of other global benefactors, the Islamics who have more than "crudely" garnished the Europeans with their black gold, not to mention a bounty of related benefits, are turning up to settle long standing accounts. Now it could come as a surprise that they might even far prefer to settle accounts in Shari'a Law!

On the other hand, just a tad of real estate will do nicely for the Ishmaelites to share the Western scenery with old trading partners, to fan out the growing family's needs and, last but not least, to foster the faith among the infidel!

Need I note that the longer the indebtedness, the higher the price tag! Poor old Antonio's pound of flesh would have been "cheap at half the price" as the old-timers where I grew up used to say.

Learning To Use an Islamic Calculator

At this *point* (again you can think *thorn*) nothing would be more apropos than some statistical excerpts from Dr. Peter Hammond's book: *Slavery, Terrorism and Islam.*[8] Most of these figures were also in an article published by *Front Page Magazine* in early 2008.[9]

Dr. Hammond tells us that:

"Islam is not only a religion nor is it a cult. It is a complete system. Islam has religious, legal, political, economic and military components. The religious component is a beard for all the other components. Islamisation occurs when there are sufficient Muslims in a country to agitate for their so-called 'religious rights.' When politically correct and culturally diverse societies agree to 'the reasonable' Muslim demands for their 'religious rights,' they also get the other components under the table.

"As long as the Muslim population remains around 1% of any given country they will be regarded as a peace-loving minority and not as a threat to anyone. In fact, they may be featured in articles and films, stereotyped for their colourful uniqueness. These countries would include: United States - Muslim 1.0%; Australia - Muslim 1.5%; Canada - Muslim 1.9%; China - Muslim 1%-2%; Italy - Muslim 1.5%; Norway - Muslim 1.8% .[10]

"At 2% and 3% they begin to proselytize from other ethnic minorities and disaffected groups with major recruiting from the (jails) and among street gangs. Some of these countries are: Denmark - Muslim 2%; Germany - Muslim 3.7%; United Kingdom - Muslim 2.7%; Spain - Muslim 4%.

"From 5% on they exercise an inordinate influence in proportion to their percentage of the population. They will push for the introduction of *halal* (clean by Islamic standards) food, thereby securing food preparation jobs for Muslims. They will increase pressure on supermarket chains to feature it on their shelves - along with threats for failure to comply. France - Muslim 8%; Sweden - Muslim 5%; Switzerland - Muslim 4.3%; Dutch - Muslim 5.5%.

"At this point, they will work to get the ruling government to allow them to rule themselves under Shari'a, the Islamic Law. The ultimate goal of Islam is not to convert the world but to establish Shari'a law over the entire world.

"When Muslims reach 10% of the population, they will increase lawlessness as a means of complaint about their conditions (e.g. Paris - car-burnings). Any non-Muslim action that offends Islam will result in uprisings and threats (e.g. Amsterdam - Mohammed cartoons). These include: India

- Muslim 13%; Israel - Muslim 16%; Kenya - Muslim 10%; Russia - Muslim 10-15%.

"After reaching 20% expect hair-trigger rioting, jihad militia formations, sporadic killings and church and synagogue burning: Ethiopia - Muslim 32.8%.

"At 40% you will find widespread massacres, chronic terror attacks and ongoing militia warfare. Some of these nations are: Bosnia - Muslim 40%; Chad - Muslim 53.1%; Lebanon - Muslim 59.7%.

"From 60% you may expect unfettered persecution of non-believers and other religions, sporadic ethnic cleansing (genocide), use of Shari'a Law as a weapon and the imposition of the Jizya, the tax placed on infidels: Albania - Muslim 70%; Malaysia - Muslim 60.4%; Qatar - Muslim 77.5%; Sudan - Muslim 70%.

"After 80% expect State run ethnic cleansing and genocide. Current examples of these are: Egypt - Muslim 90%; Gaza - Muslim 98.7%; Indonesia - Muslim 86.1%; Iran - Muslim 98%; Iraq - Muslim 97%; Jordan - Muslim 92%; Pakistan - Muslim 97%; Palestine - Muslim 99%; Syria - Muslim 90%; Turkey - Muslim 99.8%; United Arab Emirates - Muslim 96%.

"100% will usher in the peace of *Dar-es-Salaam* - the Islamic House of Peace - there's supposed to be peace because everybody is a Muslim: Afghanistan - Muslim 100%; Saudi Arabia - Muslim 100%; Somalia - Muslim 100%; Yemen-Muslim 99.9%.

"Of course, that's not the case...Muslims then start killing each other for a variety of reasons. It is good to remember that in many, many countries, such as France, the Muslim populations are centered around ghettos based on their ethnicity. Muslims do not integrate into the community at large. Therefore, (from their ghettos) they can exercise more power than their national average would indicate."

Sobering, is it not? More sobering is the fact that Dr. Hammond's book was in print already back in 2008, and *his listed data source was from the CIA World Fact Book of 2007,* which is one year older than that! As they say in Israel, one week is a long time in politics! And as the West should be noting, in the Islamic infiltration patterns into the nations, two years is even a fair bit longer!

Chillingly, the chickens of Europe are coming home—not only to roost—but actually to collect a bit more interest on the principle than chicken feed!

Looking at Ourselves

William Ewart Gladstone of 19th century vintage was elected the Prime Minister of England four times between 1868 and 1894, sort of a metronome prime minister we might say. But apparently he made a proclamation in those days that would have cost him a few more kilos of kidneys than a mere "pound of flesh" today. He viciously berated the Koran and declared, "So long as there is this book, there will be no peace in the world."[11] Poor William would be whirling like an interred dynamo today with the UK's 2.7% powerhouse of "peaceful" protesters!

But even though the massive influence of Islam is affecting today's superpowers beyond comprehension of a century ago, I don't want to get further sidetracked with details such as Jihad or Shari'a law as awesome and as gruesome as they are. I want to look at the West—a look at ourselves—who we are and what we are. What might we have been? What have we done that has gone so sour? If such as the Saudis yearn to slice off our heads and sever hands, I doubt that too much is going to change at this time of the day—perhaps we should say night. There is a verse for the end of the day that says:

And he said to me, "Do not seal the words of the prophecy of this book, for the time is at hand. He who is unjust, let him be unjust still; he who is filthy, let him be filthy still; he who is righteous, let him be righteous still; he who is holy, let him be holy still." [12]

So just taking a good look at ourselves instead of chafing at where the barbarians are heading is what is now left of what we may yet be able to fix. There are volumes already written about the horrific threats of Ishmael, Esau, and Amalek, but the United Nations' mandated Politically Correct Incitement Patrol are soon getting set to wipe the bookshelves clean of this so-called "blasphemy" (aka exposure of Islam), so what's the point to keep adding more?

Therefore, let us take a good look at ourselves as Westerners, where we as a group—as well as individually—have had our blind spots about how we really appear in the eyes of the Most High, and what we might yet do to turn our performance around a bit before His Messiah returns. As Westerners, somewhere along the line we picked up the "points system" that how many books we've written, how many Bibles we've translated, how many souls we've saved, and how many prophecies we've given are the bottom line!

Obviously these are worthy works and are not to be negated, but are they actually on the Western mindset of production, or in heaven's fellowship by participation? If we're looking for bigger numbers—be it Jew or Gentile—let's remember One who said: *"Produce fruit in keeping with repentance…For I tell you that out of these stones God can raise up children for Abraham."* [13]

But if we're looking for Family unity along with a bit of adoration of Abba—we've quoted this one a few times before, but it won't hurt to say it again: *"The King will reply, 'I tell you the truth, whatever you did for one of the least of these brothers of mine, you did for me.*"[14]

So as we take personal inventory, the Western worldview has prompted us to do some wonderful works, but perhaps the King of the Universe would be even more pleased if we garnished *all of this* with a bit more intimacy with Him!

An Endemic Anti-Semitism

So having made that point, let's finish up this chapter with Connie's Kids and most probably "Eurabia's" biggest boo-boo of all that began even before Constantine was born.

Some of the early Church Fathers that followed the Apostolic Age became bitterly anti-Semitic such as St. Ignatius of Antioch early in the 2nd century, who forbade the believers to keep the Sabbath and other matters of Hebraic heritage.

Not a few more followed in a hardening of their anti-Judaic positions in the 3rd century. Emboldened by a once-secular Emperor Constantine's unprecedented back flip in the 4th century, an additional flood of anti-Judaic postures followed suit. Slovenian born Jerome who worked some of his later years in Bethlehem was an exception during that period; however, many of his colleagues became embittered against the Jewish roots of their newfound faith.

Greek born Father John Chrysostom emerged as the "most unrelenting enemy of Judaism" of the time while Roman born Ambrose, Bishop of Milan, justified the destruction of a synagogue under his watch. And there was a Bishop Cyril, Patriarch of Alexandria of the 5th century, who incited a mob of anti-Jewish rioting in his day.[15] Lovely men of the "cloth" who were perhaps unfamiliar with Isaiah 64:6[16] since Hebrew Scriptures were well out of bounds to such holy men!

The list is too long and the anti-Semitic hatred of the developing Greco-Roman clergy of the early Church too deep to detail more of the developments. Suffice it to say that this was hardly limited to anti-Semitism, but against the Torah and remainder of the sacred Hebrew Testament as well. It must be remembered that these were the only Scriptures that Yeshua and the apostles knew and taught from, and while we dare not whitewash a hard-nosed Jewish hierarchy, it does take two to tango! Bedrock Hebrew Scriptures were out, Greco-Roman tradition was in, and hatred heralded a new highway to travel!

Jews have long acknowledged that it takes only three of their number to hold four opinions! But sadly, Constantine's kids—as we have dubbed them—must have learned that part of their spiritual heritage far better than the "spiritual stones" that build "A *Kingdom that cannot be shaken*."[17]

The despicable part is that Constantine's descendants into the Dark Ages infected Europe with an incurable anti-Semitism that even penetrated into Luther's Reformation and blighted much—but thankfully not all—of the renewed church that followed. This blind bigoted hatred of anything Jewish is undeniably the prime reason behind the inability of the Jew to recognize the role of Yeshua as any linkage whatsoever to his Father in heaven today.

If you're not Jewish, you'll never know what it is to feel this estrangement from the world at large. Yet it doesn't go away even after "those others" have all gone home. You still know it. And when a perceived holier-than-thou "religious" atmosphere comes off as an aura of censure against you or your people, the normal Jewish knee-jerk sensation is, "Get me out of here fast!" But in a Gentile world, most often there's nowhere to go. Even the more humane approach in the form of a misguided and less than biblical Western mindset to "save" them from their Jewishness is a nonstarter in any kind of a positive relationship. Neither side gets it quite right!

Redemption involves securing a relationship with Abba, and *not* a deliverance from one's ethnic roots. This would certainly seem to be a given for any race relations. But ironically, when it comes to relating to the Jew, it has always seemed to have been a bit higher hurdle for some "should-have-been-grateful" Gentiles to be able to clear the bar!

Luther in his own hierarchical upheaval had become so utterly cynical with Rome's revulsion of the Jew that he presumed the favored flock would now come flooding into his Lutheran fold. Alas, they didn't!

They had become so gun-shy of the heavy armor among those less-than-Torah taught Gentiles, they didn't come anywhere near Martin's modified manners. He soon became so disgusted with those ungrateful renegades (presumably still in the wilderness—if not Egypt) that in his later years he made an unprecedented U-turn and uttered despicable epithets against the Jews that even the worst of the former Fathers never even thought of.[18]

In some of his later sermons he actually advocated that the overly fervent of his followers even murder Jews when possible, or at least raze their shops and synagogues. Moreover, a minimum of research will verify that the Nazis actually used Luther's writings to validate their own vitriolic policies in the genocide of 6 million of their number in Hitler's gas chambers of WWII.

Even though by 1980 most of the Lutheran Church had voted to distance themselves from their founder's vicious 16th century tirades, the foment of anti-Jewish bigotry has continued to broil on among the neo-Nazis of Germany and across Europe to this day!

Eurabia, Added Anti-Semitism and the Consequences

So regrettably, what do we now have in *this day*? Added to the standoff that still lingers with a certain anti-Semitic segment of the church, Europe now has an added overwhelming tsunami of a less than Jew-loving Eurabia as we noted in the alarming statistics cited earlier.

As Islamization mounts to crisis proportions across Europe, the anti-Semitic incidents of defacing synagogues, ever so "peaceful" demonstrations featuring violence, knifings, muggings, physical abuse, and all manner of persecution is hitting a new crescendo—a subtle reminder that old Europe has been getting some new neighbors!

So after a few centuries, just as the churches across the continent finally begin to show some wisdom and responsibility, the B-Team of anti-Semitism comes into the foray—or should we say the M-Team—to harass the Jews. And by the way—you might have guessed—M hardly stands for maturity! Connie, Connie, Connie! What have you created?

And just what *all* has anti-Semitism started? Hatred, venom and violence are a few of the undesirables for starters, but looking behind the essence of *all* anti-Semitism for *all* these years, there might be a few more chickens out there heading home to the roost than we first realized.

Jews are no different than anyone else for accountability. Some may have done the right things; some may have done the opposite. Being the Chosen People means anything but getting a gold star for your efforts—unless you count those yellow stars Hitler passed out before the Jews were forced into the Nazi gas chambers!

Myriads of Abraham's offspring loathe that concept of "chosenness." Traditional targets do not prefer pedestals! Some stragglers of all stripes, on the other hand, do hope for a pedestal at times. The grass always seems to create more chlorophyll at the far end of the field! The bottom line, however, is that most of us really don't want to be different. But let's face it, friends. We're all different. Otherwise we couldn't tell our kids from the neighbors!

But being "chosen" is not an evaluation. It's an assignment. And with Abba, you don't even have to do it if you don't want to. Just wait till He shows up and see whether He gets a bit upset or not! Okay. I guess *chosen* does have its ups and downs, but it certainly isn't a peck order like it might sound at first—whether you're a pet parakeet or a prune pit!

But what I *really* want to get across is that it's not the one who's picked for a purpose that has the biggest problem. It's the one who messes with the kid who was picked to run an errand for the King of kings. Running the errand is actually back burner. That's straightforward stuff. That's life. You do it or you don't do it. If you *don't* do it—which is hardly recommended—you wait and see what happens! If you do it, no worries!

But tripping someone on Abba's assignment to post a letter so that he falls in the mud and loses the memo, is trouble big time! That's as simplistic as I can describe anti-Semitism, my friends. And that's why Abba told Abraham in Genesis 12:3:

> *I will bless those who bless you, and whoever curses you I will curse; and all peoples on earth will be blessed through you.*

And that's why a continuing anti-Semitic Europe may yet have more problems than a hen house full of Hezbollah. The first followers of those interfering with the Almighty's choice of servant is bad enough, but future repercussions may also add much more of the unexpected!

And speaking of hen houses, which actually came first, the chicken or the egg? "Christians" who were messing up God's Pilot Project? Or was it the aftermath that made room for Hezbollah and cousins? Or perhaps a little of both? The truth is there are consequences!

But it's hardly just a European moment of truth. America at the moment is paddling the same canoe, and Niagara draweth nigh!

Finally, the Most High never said there are no naughty Jews. Neither did I. The Hebrew Scriptures attest from time immemorial that God disciplines His people with divine judgment: The Assyrians, the Babylonians, Amalek, and the Philistines. But what I do insist is if the Ancient of Days sends His servant—individually or collectively—to go post a letter or run an errand, better not to fool with the Plan! Whether he gets distracted on his way to the post office or not is none of my business. Who am I *"to judge someone else's servant? To his own master he stands or falls."*[19]

It's a universal principle that Abba wants to look after the discipline in His own household. It was no different for me if outsiders tried to punish my kids when they were small. Nor was it for you with your kids. If my kids needed a bit of power steering, I'll do it. And you are the same. But most significant of all, so is the Almighty. But unfortunately Connie and the frustrated Fathers didn't know this. Nor did they probably remember that God had said:

...for I, the Lord your God, am a jealous God, punishing the children for the sin of the fathers to the third and fourth generation of those who hate me, but showing love to a thousand generations of those who love me and keep my commandments.[20]

Judgment on anti-Semitism has seen Europe burn in the past and it may not be over yet! Sorry to say the rain falls on the just and on the unjust.

Whoa, it's almost midnight—what's that cackling I hear down in the hen house at this hour? Maybe it's Hezbollah again? Or maybe it's the Messiah! Either way, let's hang in there!

[1] See: http://www.answers.com Wikipedia reference: http://www.answers.com/topic/john-iii-of-poland

[2] See: http://www.jewishvirtuallibrary.org/jsource/History/Crusader.html for one valuable source and a vast array of alternate references under http://www.answers.com/Wikipedia on *"The Crusaders."*

[3] See Victor Schlatter, *Showdown of the Gods?* (Mobile, AL: Evergreen Press, 2001), Chapter 10: *If God Loves Poor Folks, Why Not Make a Few More?"*

[4] See: http://www.answers.com Wikipedia, http://www.answers.com/john%20newton

[5] Matthew 4:4; See also Deuteronomy 8:3 and John 4:34.

[6] Revelation 4:10-11.

[7] http://www.answers.com/The%20Merchant%20of%20Venice

[8] Peter Hammond, *Slavery, Terrorism & Islam: The Historical Roots & Contemporary Threat* (Cape Town, RSA: Frontline Fellowship, 2005).

[9] *What Islam Is Not* by Dr. Peter Hammond; http://frontpagemagazine. com/Articles/Read.aspx?GUID=4DE15 EF9-A76C-4DD4-81E2-75683AEED74D

[10] To focus primarily on European percentages for our purposes, a few non-European nations have been omitted from the following statistics but can be seen in full in Hammond's book or the *Front Page Magazine* report.

[11] http://www.israelunitycoalition.org/news/article.php?id=3568

[12] Revelation 22:10-11

[13] Luke 3:8

[14] Matthew 25:40

[15] www.Answers.com/Church%20Fathers

[16] Isaiah 64:6 All of us have become like one who is unclean, and all our righteous acts are like filthy rags...

[17] Hebrews 12:28

[18] See Martin Luther: On the Jews and their Lies: http://www. awitness.org/books/luther/luther_jews/15_treat.html. Chapter15. Also: Victor Schlatter, *Where Is the Body?* (Shippensburg, PA: Destiny ImagePublishers,1999), p.58, Footnote 6.

[19] Romans 14:4

[20] Exodus 20:5-6.

CHAPTER 9

Is There a Metallurgist in the House?

Every chapter so far has been interwoven with a bit of likeness to America's current woes, welts, and worries with the long forgotten biblical kingdoms of millennia gone by. But since our subtitle is *Biblical Clues to the Rise and Fall of America,* we want to focus this next to final chapter on America itself. However, having so many intimate relationships across those United States, I want to underline explicitly that my deepest empathy in sharing my insights into these toughest of times is headed for a rescue package and hardly a whipping post.

I assure you that when there is a fire on the premises, the best news is not who started it, but precise information on where the exits are. Let's never overlook Abba!

I was born in America and was thus imbued with her catchy culture, her undeniable character, her quality education, and yet her ofttimes superficial streams of thinking. Thirty years should certainly be sufficient to set any such psyche in concrete! But perhaps not!

After 1961 the Almighty ironically transplanted me—along with my family—to an off and on 47 years of the most contrastive world scene that one could possibly conceive. It was not the sun-soaked sandy stretches of those South Pacific Islands of Paradise (of which Papua New Guinea happens to be one of them—in fact the largest one). Rather it was into the rugged mountain majesties of PNG's isolated and little known Southern Highlands. Our base did have shortwave radio contact with the world outside, but to this day, no telephone service.

I will never forget those mud-squishy trails, rain-soaked treks, uphill climbs, presumably not too far shy of the gates of glory! And I will never, ever, forget one moment of rapture crossing a mountain ridge—on my way to a village actually—and I looked up at Abba pretty personal-like, "What on earth am I doing here?" "Nothing on earth, Victor, nothing on earth!" I answered my own question almost automatically, "And I wouldn't trade it for anything!"

For seven former years as a young success-focused, ladder-climbing nuclear scientist, I had been poised to scale quite a different brand of mountain. I was with a USA blue-chip corporation, and in fact I had been doing rather well. But from what I had now sensed in a totally opposite worldview—almost another galaxy— "No way could I go back, Abba, no way!"

I often quip in my seminars that I got my advanced degrees from the same university where Moses had studied! He did his undergraduate degree at Pharaoh Tech,[1] and reckoned he was fairly top drawer at that point. So about then the Most High took him aside and suggested that he better take some advanced study on the backside of the mountain—in fact it might have been Physics 101. He showed him this bush that was burning[2] quite impressively and said: "Moshe, when you get my point on this one, I want you to see if you can find the ashes!" That should have earned him a Doctorate in Physics with added honors as a licensed tour guide in Israel!

So I can identify exactly with this kind of a divine wake-up call. I didn't get a Tour Guide license for PNG, but I did get a nice new Scrabble dictionary instead!

Enough nonsense, so now let's get serious and get on with the nitty-gritty of this chapter. It was on that remote mountain ridge and throughout the hillside villages below where I saw clearly that the land of my birth was not quite the New Jerusalem that so many of my countrymen and women might have hoped it was! Forty-seven years of insights into another world of tens of thousands of Papua New Guineans transformed into saints of the Most High presents an ego-shattering dynamic that few people are privileged to see.

I learned that my former turf of technological trinkets was hardly the most priceless product of the Almighty's ingenuity after all. It was only one of *the nations.* Let's have a look, and particularly so, after a catastrophic 2008.

The Decline of America

Eric Morey—himself an American citizen—is the leader of Messianic Congregation Kehilat Poriya, living not far from where I now write this book. Eric put together a sobering study on the spiritual decline of America spanning the last century. Bible be-lieving America has long prided itself on her high level of moral and spiritual integrity since her founding in 1776. But the loss of once taken-for-granted values ramrodded in through so-called "de-mocratic judgments" and un-American legal manipulations since the early 20th century makes hardly new headlines.

But documenting the downward decline over the century, as we can see it below, is all the more unnerving. I have copied below the 11 points of the Kehilat Poriya[3] study with only minor trun-cating of the four longer points, 1, 6, 8, and 9 for brevity within this chapter. Morey's article:

"The 20th century was the "American Century," but the seeds of America's decline began to be planted in the early part of the century.

1. 1925, Scopes "Monkey" Trial, beginning of teaching evolution in American schools.

2. 1948, McCollum vs. Board of Education, no religious instruction in public schools.

3. 1962, Engel vs. Vitale, no prayer in public schools.

4. 1973, Roe vs. Wade, made abortion legal (aka infanticide of the unborn) and easily obtainable in U.S.

5. 1980, Stone vs. Graham, Ten Commandments removed from public schools.

6. 1991, Madrid "Peace" Conference. America begins to pressure Israel to divide its Land. This brought many natural disasters upon America, as documented by John McTernan and Bill Koenig.

7. 2002, Ten Commandments ordered to be removed from Alabama Courthouse.

8. 2007, cumulative effect of materialism, consumerism and debt mentality in America:

   a. Consumer debt in 1977 was 20% of GDP;
      in 2007 120%

   b. Government debt increased by a factor of 10
      since 1980

   c. Total debt in America is $53 trillion, $175,000
      for every individual.

9. 2008, rampant greed (consumers borrowing beyond means to repay; banks giving sub-prime mortgages so they can sell them for quick profit; financial institutions creating mortgage and other derivatives for uncontrolled trading) caused economic implosion...

10. Christmas 2008: Santa Claus, Rudolph the Red-

Nosed Reindeer and Frosty the Snowman have replaced Yeshua the Messiah as the "Reason for the Season."

11. January 20, 2009: America will inaugurate as its president a man who is, at a minimum, sympathetic with Islam, and quite possibly himself a closet Muslim, a short 8 years after September 11, 2001!"

Morey's article then concludes with a final paragraph comparing America with Israel:

"All nations and civilizations in all of history, except one, have gone through a process of rising up, flourishing, and then into decline. America is no different. That one is the Jewish civilization and the nation of Israel, who, in spite of millennia of persecution; dispersion and genocide have remained strong and vibrant."

Turning to my own commentary, an integral add-on to point six above is mention of William Koenig's bestselling book *Eye to Eye*[4] which presents ten major "natural" disasters in the USA beginning in 1991. The first of the ten occurred on October 30 in what the weather watchers hailed as the *perfect storm*, and which virtually coincided with President George Bush Sr.'s early-on failed coercion of Israel to yield up her God-assigned territorial heritage to her Arab antagonists. Koenig's initial website summary of what we might dub the *Ten Plagues of Kennebunkport*, presented the first one as:

October 30, 1991: The Perfect Storm - As President George H. W. Bush is opening the Madrid (Spain) Conference to consider "land for peace" in Israel's Middle East role, the "perfect storm" develops in the North Atlantic, creating the largest waves ever recorded in that region. The storm travels 1000 miles from "east to west" instead of the normal "west to east" pattern and crashes into the New England Coast. Thirty-five foot waves crash into the Kennebunkport home of President Bush.

In his book, Koenig lists nine additional disasters, including eight physical devastations, that consisted of three hurricanes, three earthquakes, the massive Texas flood of October 1998 plus a tornado, the disgraceful Clinton-Lewinski scandal, the collapse of the Dow Jones in 1998 and a further collapse of the Dow in 1999, nearly simultaneous with one of the hurricanes and one of the earthquakes cited above.[5]

Ironically a number of the above tragic calamities all set records of catastrophic dimension. So it was a tad of tough luck— as some might say—in those eight years from Oct 30, 1991 to October 1999. I'm not so sure!

This sometime scientist has an ingrained sense of cause and effect, and has no time whatsoever for getting shortchanged in the cop-out concept of good luck or bad luck.[6] With other people, we sadly get cheated at times. That's not bad luck. That's bad business or perhaps hard knocks. If we learn our lesson, that's good. Abba, on the other hand, never gives short change.

Moreover, the science of statistics also gives us a few clues in the matter. Twisting statistics to fit your own tune ten times in a row is sheer fantasy. But when it *does* happen, it has to be Someone else fiddling His tune that is trying to tell us something!

We started at Kennebunkport, ME a few lines above. That was then followed by nine more "effects" of horrific misfortune that could have suggested that the "cause" of that first storm of reversed-natural-direction might well have had something to do with stabbing Israel in the back. But if we then carefully compare the potential "cause" circumstances surrounding the next nine debacles, what are they all about? Betraying Israel nine more times! There was a link every time!

Wait a minute. I'll revise that. Remember the analogy we made about messing up the kid who was given a letter to post for the King of the Universe? Scary stuff! So it's not about treachery to Israel a fraction so much as it is about contempt for the concerns of the Most High. The Hebrew Scriptures tell us some 85 times[7] that God is calling Abraham's family home to Jerusalem and environs in the end of days, and I doubt that the snub to Israel is half as dangerous as it is to cold-shoulder the King Himself.

If this isn't becoming crystal clear, I really think you should check out Koenig's book, or at a minimum review the *Ten Plagues Following Kennebunkport*! Cause and effect are in. And bad luck is out—way out!

Katrina Revisited

But before we go on to other worrisome winds whistling across America, Katrina—statistical storm number eleven—hadn't even yet stirred as Koenig was writing his new book.

The emotional trauma of that horrific 2005 New Orleans flood still has not been healed in the hearts and minds of most of the survivors, not to mention the monetary struggles of the destitute. Mockingly that horrendous debacle of human misery flowed directly on in the tide of the inhuman expulsion of innocent Israeli communities in the name of the "peace" of Gaza.

Prime Minister Ariel Sharon, now in oblivion to the heart-wrenching ruin he helped create, still languishes on life support in a coma now entering a fourth consecutive year. Yet who was behind it all? American President George W. Bush and his Palestinian duped Secretary of State, Condoleezza Rice. She surmised she saw the former suffering of her fellow Alabama blacks in hate seething Hamas who, quite the contrary, were merely sweltering in their own self-brewed stew boiling over into their own flames of bitterness toward Israel. It was *not* Alabama!

And what was the rationale for trashing twenty-one thriving, vibrant Jewish communities of prolific hothouses of food production touching all of Israel, family dwellings, their schools and synagogues, and some 8500 lives? They told us, "peacemaking"?

So what actually did the mindless uprooting of Gush Katif attain? Merely a chilling escalation of violence, bloodshed, and deaths of over 2000 more both Jews and Arabs over the next four years!

Added to human life, it became the senseless destruction of the market basket of Israel's—and Gaza's—$200 million per year exports of organic vegetable production. It turned both the trashed hothouses and bulldozed communities into terrorist training camps and missile launching pads to fire upon Israel some 10,000 mortars, Kassam rockets, and Grad missiles over those next four years, simply for the noblest and highest of Gazan "religious" devotion— killing Jews!

And what did the Americans get out of the greenhouse cum terrorist debacle? Hurricane Katrina—a catastrophic tragedy in 2005 of 1836 deaths and an $81.2 billion financial loss![8]

How do I know there really is a connection? Cryptic clues, godly men, and a combined witness from those who maintain contact with the breath of God from time to time.

In the Hebraic alphabet of 22 letters, each one has its own numerical value from 1 to 900 which gives some amazing word relationships and Scripture text insights when the numbers of any particular words of biblical concepts are added together. The technique is known as Gematria[9] and is a centuries old method of gaining below the surface scriptural comparisons.

Rabbi Lazer Brodi checked Katrina's numerical value in Hebrew and found it to be 374. He immediately searched for that exact numerical equivalent in Scripture text options. He found two exact matches. The first was: *"They have done you evil"* in Genesis 50:17 of an initial reference to Joseph's ten brothers, but with a corresponding current application to the 8500 Jewish refugees driven from their Gush Katif homes by their very own derelict government.

Moreover, the identical numerical 374 was also found in Exodus 14:15, "*the sea upon the land*" which hardly needs an explanation in how it relates to inundated New Orleans. Even with a more limited knowledge of Hebrew, I checked up on the good Rabbi's math. He came out 100%. One of the better tests as for verifying any academic formula is whether it works!

Something else that works in matching "cousin" languages of eons gone by is tracing *cognates,* a bit more straightforward and easily understood comparison by the layman. Katif and Katrina are cognates if we check carefully. The first three letters of each word match explicitly and the following vowel—both i's—also an exact match. But here we are not matching two dialects from time immemorial. These are two unique matches from two unique events in 2005! Say, who fished out those names anyway? It certainly wasn't the Rabbis or the linguists!

You can find even more expanded detail of the comparison of these two simultaneous disasters on my September 2005 website bulletin,[10] *Katrina's Days are Numbered*—one way by man, one way by his Maker, and both are now imbedded into history!

But a third lone cry from the wilderness in the detection of divine judgment came from Austria—far removed from Old Jerusalem or New Orleans! And it does bring Katrina right back into the bright lights of scrutiny and the blatant blindness of Political Correctness.

One Father Gerhard Wagner had been selected to become auxiliary Bishop in Linz, Austria, and a few of the more motivated self-elected scrutineers of his bishopric began taking note of his slightly unpalatable comments in a parish newsletter. Apparently he knew little about Gush Katif and Gaza, but he nevertheless was caught admiring the Almighty's creditable decisions on Katrina's divine retribution to New Orleans because of her brothels, abortion clinics, perverse parades, and an assortment of other abominations that Abba frowns on—actually for one's own good. (Unfortunately, Rabbi Brodi and I never even got this far.)

Wouldn't you know that the community rose up in horror that the good Bishop-elect would possibly make such disparaging comments about laid back sexual liaisons or concurrently also casting occultic connections with a lovely young lad like Harry Potter, that the poor man had to resign even before he was ordained.

On the one hand I readily recognize that it's very dangerous to make off the cuff judgments without some credible facts, but speaking of "off the cuff," it doesn't take too much divine depth to note that something is a wee bit wobbly when all that some of these pink paraders wear is merely the cuffs and little more! I think Father Wagner was pretty clear on his convictions.

So the Politically Correct advocates of a New World anarchy—even some from a once proper and austere Austria—add up another point or two for "free choice" until the Day of the Lord arrives to settle a few of these thorny issues with the necessary clout.

Moreover, the prophets of proprietary never were the most popular voices in town until they were able to get on the telly channels and could prophesy to the faithful of previously untold wealth instead!

The Boy Wonder

And finally, after a century of deliberately downgrading the King of the Universe, eleven natural disasters with a probability pointing directly to man-made causes—America has a youthful new president. The Boy Wonder is charismatic (in the secular sense), energetic, an effective speaker, and presumably carries a bit of loose change in his pocket. There was a promise of *change*, before the elections, but little did we realize that it was the dollars that would soon disappear with only a bit of change left for memory's sake!

In all fairness, we dare not lay this all at the feet of the new man. The downturn has been a long time in coming. But perhaps the scenario for the "change" quip above is an irony that was long set up for a much wider vulnerability.

But as far as the *wonder* aspect, multitudes of Bible believers across America now wonder what is going to happen next? I hate to say it, but we have long been warned!

These are early days in his presidency, and it would be a bit presumptuous to point too many fingers or to make too many predictions beyond what we have already said in the opening paragraphs of Chapter 1. Thus far it's not what he himself has done but rather the kind of people that he has picked to perform for him that has edged into not a few spinal columns with unprecedented chills.

He has had a Wahabbist background in his formative years of early education and his cultural affiliations of Islamic rooted Kenyan Luo tribal connections are certainly set in stone. Some of his earliest public acknowledgements once the presidency was in his grasp verified all of this. And he has been telling the Muslim world that he can well understand them because, "he has relatives that are Muslims." Yes, we were warned many times.

In most ethnic and tribal situations this could be a very positive connection. However, let's get back to my opening remarks in this chapter. My worldview was dramatically changed after the first three decades—now nearly five—of tribal identity with tens of thousands of God-fearing Bible believers who were once primitive—but now spiritually enviable—sons and daughters of the Most High. There's a mega difference! The new President's tribal ancestry contained a mix of Marxists and Muslims.[11] The tribal Waolas[12] who were central to the makeover of my own worldview and value system were 99% Christian or more. The Almighty does have preferences!

Yet some will still be fogged over, "What do you mean—same god, different approach?" Not quite!

Unfortunately that's the kind of flash-point phoniness the One Worlders who believe in no sovereign authority but themselves are spewing out like a volcano in prime time. It could even include some of their number who like to play church, or "let's pretend," or little Red-Riding Hood revisited—my, what a big Jihad book you have, Grandma!

A bit of bone fide research for the fantasy flock is to pin down any faithful Muslim. Ask *him* whether his god is the *same* as the biblical King of Zion, and then step back a bit!

Thus, Bible believers in the King of Zion, Abraham, Isaac, Jacob, and Yeshua sort of wonder. Oh boy, do they wonder!

I have done extensive research on the new president's precedents, profile, priorities, and probabilities. For further insights which I will not include in this volume, we have posted some seven bulletins on the matter on our website under "*Israel and the Nations*" between January 2007 and January 2009.[13] Sorry that some of my cryptic titles may not always give immediate clues to their target!

What Happened to that Metallurgist?

Now if we are looking at the rise and fall of America, and if we are also in the last days, it means that we had now better be looking at both of these situations simultaneously or we're going to miss out on one or the other.

There is no end-of-day's prophecy, therefore, more intriguing than Chapter 2 in Daniel where old King Nebuchadnezzar had a dream that distressed him to no end. He forgot what the dream was! All he knew was that he was upset like a pancake under construction! We touched on this a bit near the beginning of Chapter 4. The despot was going to commit astrologer-icide (I just made that up—see if you can figure it out) if his wizards and mates didn't tell him both the dream and its interpretation. Dictators are that way at times, that's why we noted back in Chapter 6 that even though democracy is not perfect, it usually has its advantages over cranky kings. But we didn't get far into the dream back in Chapter 4 so let's have a look at it now. A couple of background verses are:

The king replied to the astrologers, 'This is what I have firmly decided: If you do not tell me what my dream was and interpret it, I will have you cut into pieces and your houses turned into piles of rubble.[14]

And then their reply:

The astrologers answered the king, "There is not a man on earth who can do what the king asks! No king, however great and mighty, has ever asked such a thing of any magician or enchanter or astrologer. What the king asks is too difficult. No one can reveal it to the king except the gods, and they do not live among men." This made the king so angry and furious that he ordered the execution of all the wise men of Babylon.[15]

Well, as you might have guessed that brought Prophet Daniel into the case and he presents *not his credentials*, but those of his Boss:

...but there is a God in heaven who reveals mysteries. He has shown King Nebuchadnezzar what will happen in days to come. Your dream and the visions that passed through your mind as you lay on your bed are these: As you were lying there, O king, your mind turned to things to come, and the revealer of mysteries showed you what is going to happen.[16]

And here's the dream:

You looked, O king, and there before you stood a large statue— an enormous, dazzling statue, awesome in appearance. The head of the statue was made of pure gold, its chest and arms of silver, its belly and thighs of bronze, its legs of iron, its feet partly of iron and partly of baked clay. While you were watching, a rock was cut out, but not by human hands. It struck the statue on its feet of iron and clay and smashed them. Then the iron, the clay, the bronze, the silver and the gold were broken to pieces at the same time and became like chaff on a threshing floor in the summer. The wind swept them away without leaving a trace. But the rock that struck the statue became a huge mountain and filled the whole earth.[17]

And finally we get the interpretation of the dream, which included Babylon's present head-of-gold rule. Below that is a silver-symbolized, two-armed Medo-Persian empire, followed by a Greek represented torso of bronze.[18] A Rome representation of legs that are made of iron, signals the longest and the strongest segment of the statue, and thus the longest reign or influence of all five kingdoms. And finally we have the feet and clay symbolism of the end of days:

This was the dream, and now we will interpret it to the king. You, O king, are the king of kings. The God of heaven has given you dominion and power and might and glory; in your hands he has placed mankind and the beasts of the field and the birds of the air. Wherever they live, he has made you ruler over them all. You are that head of gold. After you, another kingdom will rise, inferior to yours. Next, a third kingdom, one of bronze, will rule over the whole earth. Finally, there will be a fourth kingdom, strong as iron—for iron breaks and smashes everything—and as iron breaks things to pieces, so it will crush and break all the others. Just as you saw that the feet and toes were partly of baked clay and partly of iron, so this will be a divided kingdom; yet it will have some of the strength of iron in it, even as you saw iron mixed with clay. As the toes were partly iron and partly clay, so this kingdom will be partly strong and partly brittle. And just as you saw the iron mixed with baked clay, so the people will be a mixture and will not remain united, any more than iron mixes with clay.[19]

There is mind-boggling symbolism in the dream which spans the centuries up to this day. Gold is the wealthiest kingdom but structurally the softest, i.e. weakest metal. Silver signifying Cyrus' Persian rule had a lower metallic value but is physically stronger; bronze becomes a much more sturdy material for construction but has no comparison economically to the two previous metals. And the iron legs are the strongest and longest of all, representing both Rome's superior military might as well as the longest duration of power for any of the five kingdoms. But with regard to the comparative value, iron is obviously better for bridges than for bracelets!

And finally the feet of iron and clay are a graphic image for not only America, but the end-of-days devastations now inundating the entire globe. The military might of today's global nuclear hegemony—the iron aspect—is enough to reduce planet earth to cinders a few times. But alas! The feet and very end-of-days toes are the clay[20] of political instability, along with worldwide cultural and moral decadence.

Moreover we should also take note of the Most High's precision in His symbolism. There are two legs and two feet to remind us that Rome was a kingdom of a long-term division between an Eastern and a Western kingdom. But no less are the clay and iron feet of today's world culturally cloven along identical lines between a technological West and a medieval if not barbaric East!

In the time of those kings, the God of heaven will set up a kingdom that will never be destroyed, nor will it be left to another people. It will crush all those kingdoms and bring them to an end, but it will itself endure forever. This is the meaning of the vision of the rock cut out of a mountain, but not by human hands—a rock that broke the iron, the bronze, the clay, the silver and the gold to pieces. The great God has shown the king what will take place in the future. The dream is true and the interpretation is trustworthy.[21]

So there it is, America! It's going to be an exciting time to be alive if watching the Rock of Ages roll in happens to be one of your prize priorities, that is.

Isaiah put it this way:

So this is what the Sovereign Lord says: "See, I lay a stone in Zion, a tested stone, a precious cornerstone for a sure foundation; the one who trusts will never be dismayed. I will make justice the measuring line and righteousness the plumb line..."[22]

And Zechariah 12:3 pictures the Rock as one might view it from the Mount of Olives to the east:

On that day, when all the nations of the earth are gathered against her, I will make Jerusalem an immovable rock for all the nations. All who try to move it will injure themselves.

But make no mistake; the vision is of all *world* kingdoms at the final trumpet in the end of days.[23]

The seventh angel sounded his trumpet, and there were loud voices in heaven, which said: "The kingdom of the world has become the kingdom of our Lord and of his Messiah, and he will reign forever and ever."

But there is an infinite difference between *world* kingdoms and *world* overcomers.[24]

I have told you these things, so that in me you may have peace. In this world you will have trouble. But take heart! I have overcome the world.

So keep that difference handy. The Ancient of Days will never tread on those end-of-days clay toes of His beloved!

---

[1] See Acts 7:22. "Moses was educated in all the wisdom of the Egyptians and was powerful in speech and action."

[2] See the complete account in its formal biblical presentation in Exodus 3.

3 See http://www.kehilatporiya.org Kehilat Poriya, Tveria, Israel: *The Decline of America,* Jan 2009.

4 Bill Koenig, *Eye to Eye: Facing the Consequences of Dividing Israel* (About Him Publishing, Alexandria, VA, 2006).

5 The summary of all 10 of the of bizarre disasters are listed in *Katrina: Additions and Corrections* Bulletins: http://www.spim.org.au/bulletins/1405.doc Scroll down to midway in the Bulletin: TEN MAJOR EVENTS.

6 For biblical logic into "chance" see *Essence of 2300* Bulletin: http://www.spim.org.au/bulletins/708.doc

7 See http://www.spim.org.au/bulletins/307.doc

8 http://en.wikipedia.org/wiki/Hurricane_Katrina

9 See *Encyclopedia of Judaism* on http://www.answers.com/ topic/gematria

10 See http://www.spim.org.au/bulletins/1305.doc

11 Research abounds on his Kenyan roots and political relationships with cousin Raila Odinga and readily found on Google or Answers.com. Personal research is cached on www.israelunitycoalition.org/ news/article.php?id=2998; www.spim.org.au/bulletins/808.doc; www.spim.org.au/bulletins/208.doc; and www.spim.org.au/bulletins/1308.doc.

12 See: http://www.spim.org.au/article5.htm *"Third World Awakening— Greek Roadblocks or a Hebraic Road,* Nov 2004.

13 See *Israel and the Nations* 2007 through 2009 on http://www.spim.org.au.

14 Daniel 2:5

15 Daniel 2:10-12

16 Daniel 2:28-29

17 Daniel 2:31-35

18 As we will note in Chapter 10, bronze being inferior to gold and silver, most frequently is a representation of man or servant hood. It is remarkable that Greece as represented by Bronze in the vision, has been the original source of humanism—the worship of man.

19 Dan 2:36-43

20 Of special note should be the Creator's expertise in His creating from clay, and why it suggests vulnerability in the end of days. See Genesis 2:7

21 Daniel 2:44-45

22 Isaiah 28:16-17a

23 Revelation 11:15

24 John 16:33

CHAPTER 10

The Nation Not Numbered

No other Scripture is as explicit in identifying Israel as the world's oldest hatred as the first eight verses of Psalm 83:

*O God, do not keep silent; be not quiet, O God, be not still. See how **your enemies** are astir, how **your foes** rear their heads. With cunning **they** conspire against your people; **they** plot against those you cherish. "Come," **they** say, "let us destroy them as a nation, that the name of Israel be remembered no more." With one mind **they** plot together; **they** form an alliance against you—the tents of Edom and the Ishmaelites, of Moab and the Hagrites, Gebal, Ammon and Amalek, Philistia, with the people of Tyre. Even Assyria has joined **them** to lend strength to the descendants of Lot* (emphasis added).

And final verses 17 and 18 of Psalm 83 chime in with a ring of truth for a final sovereignty of the King of the Universe over that hate-fest of Middle East rebellion:

*May **they** ever be ashamed and dismayed; may **they** perish in disgrace. Let **them** know that you, whose name is the Lord— that you alone are the Most High over all the earth"* (emphasis added).

So let's do a little investigation. In the two mentions of "God's foes" above, followed up with nine bolded references to *they* or *them*, just who may *they* happen to be? In the opening Scripture we see *them* identified as ten ho-hum Bible names of bygone memory

from Sunday School—if you even went to Sunday School.
Otherwise they are Bible trivia that the unchurched may do well to
have heard of even three of them! The only thing, however, that we
must note is the bottom line of what these ten clans held in
common: It was that the Jews were anything but their favorite
friends and neighbors! So why not try to match this more than
three millennia-old mindset with our current 21st century?

• For *"tents of Edom"* just read: *South Jordan.*
• For *Ishmaelites* read: *Saudi Arabia.*
• For *Moab* read: *Middle Jordan.*
• For *Hagrites*: *Saudi Arabia* again—they've got a bit of oil now
which has changed nothing!
• For *Gebal* it's: *Lebanon.*
• For *Ammon* read: *North Jordan* and *South Syria.*
• For *Amalek*[1] (grandson of Esau) read: lower *Jordan* and upper
Saudi Arabia.
• For *Philistia*, substitute *Gaza.* (The ancient Philistines died out,
but the Arabs noted the name as useful and recycled it!)
• For the people of *Tyre*: Try *South Lebanon* again.
• For *Assyria* read: *Iraq.*

That's all ten! "The children of Lot" refer to Moab and
Ammon, which merely takes us back to Jordan.

So from 2009 we backtrack three millennia or more and ask:
What else is new?

Another question: What makes these Arab entities hate their
nice Jewish neighbors so much? Is it Jewish culture and manner-
isms? Possibly, yet that has changed enormously over the eons. Is it
jealousy? Quite probably. What about the decisions of the Abba of
Abraham? Getting warmer!

The King of Creation who started making friends with
Abraham brought a bit of baggage with Him—monotheism! And
that in turn taunted an enemy tailing Him in the shadows, that

guru of deception from Eden's ancient garden.[2] He cherished neither a sovereign Creator's choices of companions nor His mandate of who had the last word. And *that* set the stage for battle! Eventually a couple of problem kids also appeared in the family of promise—namely Ishmael and Esau who each finished *second* in their day. This in turn inspired some "ideas" of their own, and thus it began!

Ironically even then the family feud didn't get too bad until the 7th century AD when the tents of Ishmael came up with an entirely new competitive code, complete with a coup d'état to replace Abba, and that was it! So there we are, and if you are on reasonable terms with the Ancient of Days, you can see where it is that we are now!

Obviously I'm skimming ever so sketchily but this is actually a fair overview of the ten left-fielders of Psalm 83. And after almost four millennia, we're back to our question: What else is new? For the Family as a whole, there's a lot of Good News since then, but so far for the Middle East muddle: Not much!

Israel's Fleeting Friends

Moreover, there are not a few newcomers to take sides in the spat. The tears and trauma in Edom's tents now woos a lot of new sympathizers on their side. They have managed to enlist an added 57 votes—religion-wise basically—on to those initial ten troubled hearts to make a solid 57 member bloc in the United Nations. A roughly 30% solidarity in the some 200 member world body gives a fairly hefty influence to give even added strength to the "descendants of Lot."

The only hope left, therefore, for the descendants of Abraham, Isaac, and Jacob is Psalm 83:18: *"Let them know that you, whose name is the Lord—that you alone are the Most High over all the earth."*

Now the Most High is not a bad ally to have on your side. Yet on that other side, those fans of fair weather following keep getting fewer and fewer!

The tighter Israel gets squeezed in their tiny tract—a land ratio of a mere 1 to 600 with their near Arab neighbors—the more they struggle to survive. Granted, they do have a fair bit of fire power from their surrounded setting. But the more they use it to defend themselves, the fewer friends they have elsewhere because it goofs up the cash flow in global trade, including that petrol thing. And if it hits their back pocket, that's when Europe goes a bit bonkers, not to mention America and the rest of the big bidders. Recent statistics show that anti-Semitism in Europe is higher now than any time since 1938, so we might consider adding the EU to Psalm 83 as well!

So let's go to America. A recent article on Israel's Christian friends by veteran columnist Michael Freund[3] reports that there are some 100,000 active Christian Zionists in America, and even twice that many entire churches who are committed to pray for Israel. So Israel does have a few friends left who look above and beyond her frailties and frequent secular unfaithfulness to her God's perpetual plans for this ancient Family honed for His purposes.

But unfortunately, though these faithful do have some limited clout in the Congress, the echo becomes much more of a whisper in the White House, because when you get to that pedestal of power, either you don't have time to mess with incidentals like Psalm 83 or you become over-taxed with more mundane matters like global profits, petrol pumps, or prestige among *the nations*. It's weird, but this *always* seems to lead to making peace between the Jews and the Arabs! The secret's out! This too is tied to trade, prosperity, and big bucks, and you get too busy to toy with any lesser level of lunacy!

Now sit down and think a moment. The last six American presidents have all set their sights on ending some 4000 years of vitriol between two ancient families that forever and a day have mixed like oil and water or melded like chalk and cheese. And the audacious irony is that they *must* do it in four years or less! They should know by now that they will never make it in eight years or even eighty unless they happen to opt to run for anti-Christ in the interim. And should this be the case their success rate could be 100% for the first three-and-a-half years, but anything beyond that we *carefully* watch the walls of Jerusalem!

But back to the moment, can you imagine that even from the highest pedestal and the most powerful position on the globe, a mere politician thinks that he can mend a 4000-year rift in a few years? We didn't say smartest, did we?

I must have quoted him in every book I have written when I cite philosopher George Santayana: "Those who cannot remember the past are condemned to repeat it."[4] So much for the most potent pillars of *the nations*! And so much for the most valiant aspirations of the people who elected them!

If you haven't noticed so far—and if we get nowhere else in these pages—I'd like to get your eyes a wee bit higher than the humanity trodden streets on which we walk! Never depend on the politicians for what Abba can and will do much better!

Words of Wisdom From out of the Woodwork

But now let's hear from a few of the fellows who spent precious little time in which we might call the halls of holiness, but nonetheless somehow penetrated the realm of reality.

Probably the most unlikely of all was crusty old Balaam, a soothsayer from upstream Euphrates in Mesopotamia. In our day and time this is the place where the Euphrates crosses the Syrian-Turkish border. It was undoubtedly the awe of the Almighty which inspired his prophetic utterance as he surveyed the multitudes of Israel from afar:

From the rocky peaks I see them; from the heights I view them. I see a people who live apart and do not consider themselves one of the nations. Who can count the dust of Jacob or number the

fourth part of Israel? Let me die the death of the righteous, and
may my end be like theirs![5]

Then there was that legend of literature—who himself was little likely to credit the Most High with much in the way of majesty—the memorable Mark Twain. Yet he was mightily impressed with what he saw down on the earth in the unbreakable spirit of the Jew.

> "The Jews constitute but one percent of the human race...Properly the Jew ought hardly to be heard of; but he is heard of, has always been heard of. He is as prominent on the planet as any other people...He has made a marvelous fight in this world, in all the ages; and he has done it with his hands tied behind him...The Egyptian, the Babylonian, and the Persian rose, filled the planet with sound and splendor, then faded to dream-stuff and passed away; the Greek and the Roman followed, and made a vast noise, and they are gone; other peoples have sprung up and held their torch high for a time, but it burned out, and they sit in twilight now, or have vanished. The Jew saw them all, beat them all, and is now what he always was...All things are mortal but the Jew; all other forces pass, but he remains. What is the secret of his immortality?" [6]

And then there was the anecdote of Britain's Queen Victoria asking 19th century Prime Minister Benjamin Disraeli, "What evidence can you give me of the existence of God?" to which Disraeli responded, "The Jew, your majesty, the Jew."

Finally, one more legendary bit of biblical brilliance was the literary masterpiece of the Dry Bones of Ezekiel 37:

The hand of the LORD was upon me, and he brought me out
by the Spirit of the LORD and set me in the middle of a valley;
it was full of bones. He led me back and forth among them, and

I saw a great many bones on the floor of the valley, bones that were very dry. He asked me, "Son of man, can these bones live?" I said, "O Sovereign LORD, you alone know." [7]

And Ezekiel prophesied as he was commanded:

So I prophesied as I was commanded. And as I was prophesying, there was a noise, a rattling sound, and the bones came together, bone to bone. I looked, and tendons and flesh appeared on them and skin covered them, but there was no breath in them. [8]

And he prophesied once more:

Come from the four winds, O breath, and breathe into these slain, that they may live. So I prophesied as he commanded me, and breath entered them; they came to life and stood up on their feet—a vast army. Then he said to me: "Son of man, these bones are the whole house of Israel." [9]

And the Almighty Himself said:

O my people, I am going to open your graves and bring you up from them; I will bring you back to the land of Israel. Then you, my people, will know that I am the LORD, when I open your graves and bring you up from them. I will put my Spirit in you and you will live, and I will settle you in your own land. Then you will know that I the LORD have spoken, and I have done it, declares the LORD. [10]

Ezekiel painted the word pictures for us. But it was the King of Creation Himself who designed Israel—both a beacon of brilliance, yet limited in his days to bones and flesh. It was the Most High's masterpiece to first design, then to create, then to wrestle to a surrender,[11] and in finality, to perfect and redeem in the end of days. It marks both the man and the nation that bore his name.

Secret Survivors for Something Special

But before we leave this chapter, Ezekiel gives us one more prophecy—slightly less graphic but nonetheless a memorable metaphor that is reserved for our times. We touched on this in my earlier book, *Where is the Body?*, now a decade back into history.[12] Today the mushrooms of a long-hidden people seem to be popping up and out faster than ever. Let's have a look at a bit of troublesome text for some of the saints—mind boggling for others:

The word of the LORD came to me: Son of man, take a stick of wood and write on it, "Belonging to Judah and the Israelites associated with him." Then take another stick of wood, and write on it, "Ephraim's stick, belonging to Joseph and all the house of Israel associated with him." Join them together into one stick so that they will become one in your hand. When your countrymen ask you, "Won't you tell us what you mean by this?" say to them, "This is what the Sovereign LORD says: I am going to take the stick of Joseph—which is in Ephraim's hand—and of the Israelite tribes associated with him, and join it to Judah's stick, making them a single stick of wood, and they will become one in my hand." Hold before their eyes the sticks you have written on and say to them, "This is what the Sovereign LORD says: I will take the Israelites out of the nations where they have gone. I will gather them from all around and bring them back into their own land. I will make them one nation in the land, on the mountains of Israel. There will be one king over all of them and they will never again be two nations or be divided into two kingdoms. They will no longer defile themselves with their idols and vile images or with any of their offenses, for I will save them from all their sinful backsliding, and I will cleanse them. They will be my people, and I will be their God. My servant David will be king over them, and they will all have one shepherd. They will follow my laws and be careful to keep my decrees."[13]

So what does that all mean? Like most matters of theological vintage, for the Jews if you have three Rabbis you'll get four opinions—I think I said that a few chapters back. For the Gentiles on the other hand, you have one "Good News" and thirty-one churches to preach it—each with his own flavor of course! Never mind, Abba has a lot of different flowers in His garden and some smell better than others! And He knows weed varieties even better than you and I do—clever as we are!

So back to our *two sticks* and *one King* texts: What *is* this about? Some of the brethren believe this *all* happened *before* the Romans ran the Jews out of Jerusalem almost 2000 years ago. Certainly it is true that *all* the tribes were represented when Hezekiah celebrated the long overdue Passover in 2 Chronicles 30. But Ezekiel says "*one King*" in Chapter 37:22:

> *I will make them one nation in the land, on the mountains of Israel. There will be one king over all of them and they will never again be two nations or be divided into two kingdoms.*

Was Hezekiah that "*one King*"? Or is it someone else? There are not a few ideas on this one floating around like fluffy clouds in springtime. There also has been a lot of research done, not to mention a bit of speculation, some of which can hardly be denied. It may well be that those "Lost Tribes" are becoming divinely groomed to come home!

For information for the less than learned in the Scriptures, in 724-722 BC Shalmaneser King of Assyria captured Samaria[14]—and masses of the Northern Kingdom, aka Ephraim—were carried off to be exiled in Assyria. The numbers were never mentioned and most were never heard of again having mixed with the Assyrians. But did they totally disappear? Most probably not!

Dubbed the "Lost Tribes," much speculation about where they went has always been an intrigue. Some thought that an impressive number ended up in Britain, and much mileage is made in legends, cults, and curiosity in these matters. Others were presumed to have made it as far as Scandinavia, while yet others up to Russia, the Soviet Republics, and all across Central Europe, which has turned out to be the most realistic of all. Each one, mind you, has his own stories to stake his claim and now even DNA (stands for Do Not Argue perhaps!) has come to the fore. There are many credible books that have been written on these matters—some better than others obviously—and I shall not take a detour into the various research at this point of our journey.

The bottom line is that not a few Europeans with a bit of reflection, genealogy, and introspection find themselves with probable Hebraic linkages from way back. In fact, from my own Anabaptist background, which has a significant identity right across central Europe, noteworthy Hebraisms are being found that you wouldn't believe. I should note that there could be a few *traditional* theologians that may not believe it either! On the one hand, religious fences are not hastily mended; but on the other, these are early days of surprises, and the jury perhaps is still out.

Nevertheless, there is new information surfacing on the hour among the saints! For some, it's so what? There is always the Olive Tree adoption of Romans 11 for the Gentiles who have entered or are entering the Family of Promise, so what does it matter?

But for the Third World, those speculations in Europe and the West are perhaps but a pinhead. Most non-Jews haven't even begun to note some of the probabilities from Latin America to Southeast Asia to all of Africa for latent Hebrew heritage. Nor would they care.

A Bit More Bible

There is a fascinating verse in Jeremiah 16:14-15:

However, the days are coming, declares the Lord, when men will no longer say, "As surely as the Lord lives, who brought the Israelites up out of Egypt," but they will say, "As surely as the Lord lives, who brought the Israelites up out of the land of the

north and out of all the countries where he had banished them."
For I will restore them to the land I gave their forefathers.

A few questions: Is this what happened in 1948 when all the Sephardic Jews[15] poured out of the Islamic countries back to Israel after the UN in one small mindset of impartiality gave Israel back her ancient homeland? It was a fragmented fraction of her ancient homeland we should say!

Or was this what happened in the 1990s when about one million Russian Jews—"lost tribers" possibly—poured back into Israel including the likes of renowned Prisoner of Zion, Natan Sharansky, current Foreign Minister Avigdor Lieberman, and refusenik "Guardian Angel" Ida Nudel?

Or isn't it finished yet? This is all yours to answer. Only the "guardians of the agenda" for these matters know for sure so that frees up all the rest of us Watchmen on the Walls to keep our eyes on the walls of Jerusalem.[16]

The Hidden Harvest

But I promised you I had much more on the Messianic Mushroom Harvest! Back in the 1990s we organized tours for some 500 South Pacific Island Pilgrims across the decade to visit Jerusalem and see their Bible come alive. During the 1991 tour I had a unique experience when I dropped into the office of the photographer for the International Christian Embassy Jerusalem. Bud Burton had 1001 old photos that like any good cameraman, he couldn't bear to part with. Thus he had a vast collage of his life's legacy spread all across the back wall of his work space. And right in the center of his posted toils were photos of three dark-skinned girls that looked tauntingly familiar. "Bud, where did you take the photos of these Papua New Guinean girls?" I queried. Surprise! He told me, "They're not Papua New Guineans. They're Ethiopian Jews!"

I couldn't believe it! It just so happened that my tour had an afternoon off so I shot over to the hotel about fifteen minutes away and found three of my fellow travelers lounging in their room. They just happened to be Highlanders from the tribal language adjacent to where we had worked for three decades. I bade them to follow me for a unique something, but didn't tell them what. I presumed they would also fall into my initial notion that the trio were indeed from Papua New Guinea—glamorized in travel brochures as the "Land of the Unexpected."

On seeing the photos, their response was *more* than unexpected. They "identified" the first one as a Pangia girl, Pangia being an area some 100 km from our Base. The next one was pegged as a surety for the folks from around Mendi, our provincial capital, a mere 50 km away. They fumbled on identifying the third. "We're not sure—she must be from the coast," that is, people groups ethnically distinct from the Highland tribes."

I dropped the news. They were three young daughters all from one Jewish-African family located some 10,000 miles away! That opened an immediate reflection back to their long disregarded roots.

The eldest of my three tribal friends told me that their chief ancestor as far back as tribal tales could tally—no Alzheimer's here—was "Avram" Pamu. I wouldn't have a clue for Pamu possibilities, but Avram[17] does ring a bell, does it not? This Head of all headmen taught them not to steal, not to kill, not to take another man's wife, and not to tell lies, "but the white man came and we lost all this!"

I hesitate to think that they lost the lot. They had turned out to be God-fearing, morally motivated members of humanity, including recognition of four of Sinai's ten commandments, but what I think they "lost" after some five decades of Western contact was a realistic reckoning of their roots.

But there were other linkages than Father Avram. Both my language group (Waola) and theirs (Hela) had similar tribal legends of uncanny Genesis themes. There were minor linguistic links with Hebrew[18] as well as cross-cultural Hebraic practices.[19] Much more of the intriguing details are on our website as keyed in the endnotes.

But there is even a more far-reaching spread than those two adjacent tribal groups in the rugged Southern Highlands. Another educated young man from the Republic of Vanuatu had been reading some of my finds and became most excited about parallel comparative discoveries in his own islands.

In the early 1940s, Presbyterian Missionary Dr. J. Graham Miller wrote up findings of the earliest 19th century missionaries in what had then been the New Hebrides. Two different tribes told those early pioneers that the name of their "high god" (prior to Western contact) was *Yehova Ariki* in one of the tribes; and on the alternate island some 500 km distant, the other tribe had identified their "high God" as *Iehowa Asori*.

I have since learned that *Ariki* is the word for *king* in a related Cook Island language, and one can only presume that *Asori* means the same but in the other dialect. But the real shocker is that my "pagan" spelling checker suggested that both Yehova and Iehowa be spelled with a "J" signaling a composite "King Jehovah" rendition by the unbiased if not naive onlookers to our discovery. And one more tantalizing tad of Hebraism is that *both* of the above noted tribes practiced male circumcision, as did not a few of the Papua New Guinea tribes 3000 km to the northwest. And the Solomon Islands, another archipelago lying between these two island nations have even more to add to the stories.

So where are we heading with this material? Back to wandering Ephraim ben Joseph, that is Ephraim son of Joseph, pride and joy of his father Jacob? Perhaps, but not exactly!

Now I am a firm believer that the Most High said what He meant and meant what He said, aka inspired Scriptures. But as an earthbound translator myself, I am well aware that we translators can make misjudgments from time to time. One reason for this fragility of facts is that in every language we have words that may have a few different—even unrelated—meanings. And should this be the case, we have to translate at times by the context. Moreover, on occasion the context may not be clear, as is the case of Exodus 13:18:

> *So God led the people around by the desert road toward the Red*
> *Sea. The Israelites went up out of Egypt **armed for battle.***

The Mishnah,[20] has picked up on one such instance. The Sages say that they could not have gone out *armed for battle*—at that stage of the journey anyway—because they were slaves and slaves had no weapons. They had a valiant leader, Moshe, and an Almighty God, but no weapons!

Therefore a far more logical rendition, they conclude, is an alternate meaning of the Hebrew word: *one-fifth*. That is, only one-fifth or a mere 20% left with Moses. That makes sense. Yet I do have a problem with what the Sages suggest happened to the remaining 80%—namely that they all perished during the Plague of Three Days' Darkness. Darkness isn't exactly that lethal!

So I see not only one problem, but a *few* problems on the logistics and—pardon my daring—I also have an alternate opinion, since neither the good Rabbis nor I happened to be there at the time to trace their tracks nor nail down the numbers. I can most easily concur with that update in translation. But I find it far more realistic that after many more days of suffering under Pharaoh's foremen, the formerly fearful finally got fed up with the leeks, garlic[21] and Pharaoh, and took off for destinations unknown—like Southeast Asia and beyond.

When we Google "Lost Tribes" in the literature, we also get some very credible conclusions that take us a bit farther than England, Scandinavia, Russia, and Europe!

There are also Hebraic hints for a portion of the Afghani people with links through Pakistan or even Japan. China is another find. But these are not necessarily the ones who Shalmaneser took via Nineveh. Some may have drifted off through Babylon, as well as other of those 80% who didn't relish risking it with Moses. Yet others—whatever their tracks from the tents of Jacob—are that tsunami of Marano Jews out of Spain and Portugal that are now bubbling to the surface across Latin America! Onetime Maranos are awakening with a host now dreaming of Home!

A few specifics are the tribe of Bnei Menashe, some 5000-6000 practicing Jews from the northeast reaches of India which happens to be a smallish segment of the larger Kuki tribe numbering 1.5 million.[22] Not a few of these are trying to make aliyah back to Israel under the blessing of a number of high profile Israelis who have visited them.

And then there are the some 7 million of the inhumanely persecuted Karen tribe of eastern Myanmar[23] many of whom were formerly animist-cum-Christian tribespeople. They have from ages past maintained that they are from long lost Hebraic roots. Due to intense treachery of the Burmese military regime, some 85,000 have escaped to refugee camps in Thailand. Are they Jews? They certainly know what it is to suffer! I have personally spoken with some of them.

And finally there is Africa. The tens of thousands of Ethiopians—called Abyssinians at times—are a given. A high percentage has already returned to Israel. And one additional credible claim for bona fide African Hebraism is the Lemba tribe of South Africa.[24]

Hebraic-oriented Sabbath keeping across tribal Africa appears to have been as generic—or even more so—than the later overlay of the Western Sunday tradition.

"The Sabbath Legacy of Ethiopians is well known but the Sabbath legacy of many other African tribes in Central and West Africa are being uncovered and discovered through biblical, historical, archeological...ethnographical, anthropological, geographical, scientific and not least of all genetic evidences. The phenomenal discoveries...have confirmed the Hebraic origins and Sabbath legacy of many African tribes, a fact always known and acknowledged by Africans themselves—especially in many of their oral histories."[25]

Hailed as a "Historic Day for Black African Jews" on July 11, 2008, Uganda hosted the first ever gathering of African Jewish Communities:[26]

"The Pan-African Jewish Alliance (PAJA) held its first multi-national meeting on July 11, 2008 with participants from Jewish communities in Uganda, Zimbabwe, Nigeria, Ethiopia, Ghana, Kenya, and the United States. The representatives from African Jewish communities gathered in Uganda to celebrate with Rabbi Gershom Sizomu on the occasion of his installation as community rabbi by Conservative rabbis from the United States."

A Greater Israel Panics the Politicians

So what's it all mean? Some of these far out clutches of population may just be a pittance, just a handful. But others are in the millions. And some of these Third World hands hold a lot of other hands! Especially in Latin America; especially in Africa; even in India and China!

Certainly Israel's secular government could get a little nervous over all of this. Maybe? Maybe not! It's more likely that it's the theologians—Judaic or Christian—that would even get more bent out of shape! How can we ever shoehorn them into what we maintain we already know!

Nor did we mention those regimes of Iran, Iraq, Syria, Lebanon, Jordan, or the neo-headhunters of Hizbullah and Gaza would even get far more panicky over the possibilities. Indeed!

Suppose those Scriptures about Israel are actually true after all? Let's face it; the majority of the Westerners who play church don't *really* believe them! Neither do half the Jews in Israel, nor the some 70% of the Jews in America who voted for Obama. They don't believe that stuff! Where would you even put that many multi-racial Jews even if the Book were true?[27]

Here's where:

> *On that day the Lord made a covenant with Abram and said, "To your descendants I give this land, from the river of Egypt to the great river, the Euphrates..."*[28]

And finally, here's another verse that we might consider:

> *After this I looked and there before me was a great multitude that no one could count, from every nation, tribe, people and language, standing before the throne and in front of the Lamb. They were wearing white robes and were holding palm branches in their hands. And they cried out in a loud voice: "Salvation belongs to our God, who sits on the throne, and to the Lamb."*[29]

Then in case you may have forgotten where in the world the Almighty is going to reconstruct heaven, here's the plan:

> *I saw the Holy City, the new Jerusalem, coming down out of heaven from God, prepared as a bride beautifully dressed for her husband. And I heard a loud voice from the throne saying, "Now the dwelling of God is with men, and he will live with them. They will be his people, and God himself will be with them and be their God."*[30]

As we may recall, Barack Hussein Obama did make some great promises for change. Ironically the Ancient of Days made His promises first. I think I'll wait three or four more years for His!

By now you know my mindset is only "Abba"—not on *the nations*, not on the superpowers, not on the politicians, and certainly not on Obama. The final chapter is God, God, God—all the way!

Moreover, from the Tabernacle in the Wilderness to the Temple on the Mountain top, from the Sanhedrin of the Sages to the seminaries of the scholars, the Almighty never answers to theology; theology—just like those kings of the earth—always must answer to God!

And last of all, who knows how massive this Greater Israel dimension is going to get? I think that's why the King of the Universe inspired Jeremiah to pen:

> *This is what the Lord says, he who appoints the sun to shine by day, who decrees the moon and stars to shine by night, who stirs up the sea so that its waves roar—the Lord Almighty is his name: "Only if these decrees vanish from my sight," declares the Lord, "will the descendants of Israel ever cease to be a nation before me."*[31]

See you in the New Jerusalem!

—*Victor*

[1] See Exodus 17:16 and Deuteronomy 25:17-19 for God's historical perspective.

[2] Genesis 3:1-5.

[3] http://www.israelunitycoalition.org/news/article.php?id=3807

[4] George Santayana, *The Life of Reason or Phrases of Human Progress*, 82; (Charles Scribner's Sons, New York, 1954)

[5] Numbers 23:9-10

[6] Mark Twain, *The Complete Essays of Mark Twain*, Charles Neider, ed. (New York: Doubleday, 1963) p. 249 .

[7] Ezekiel 37:1-3

[8] Ezekiel 37:7-8

[9] Ezekiel 37: 9b-11a

[10] Ezekiel 37:12b-14

[11] See Jacob and the Angel of the Lord in Genesis 32:22-32.

[12] See Victor Schlatter, *Where Is the Body?* (Shippensburg, PA: Destiny Image Publishers,1999), Chapter 7 "Is There Life After…Constantine?"

[13] Ezekiel 37:15-24

[14] See 2 Kings Chapter17

[15] On 29 November 1947 in a moment of unprecedented favor to Israel, the UN voted to return to them a tiny slice of their original homeland. This gave a flood of Sephardic Jews exiled in Arab lands, freedom to return to Israel, while concurrently masses of Arabs fled their homes in Israel out of panic, only to end up in refugee camps, barred politically from Arab lands. See also *Who Occupies Whose Land?* http://www.spim.org.au/article4.htm

[16] Isaiah 62:6-7

[17] See Genesis 17:5

[18] See: http://www.spim.org.au/article8.htm

[19] See: http://www.spim.org.au/article6.htm

[20] A credible Scripture Commentary by the Sages. See *Mishnah* under Answers.com.

[21] Num. 11:5 *"We remember the fish we ate in Egypt at no cost—also the cucumbers, melons, leeks, onions and garlic."*

[22] See http://www.bneimenashe.com/history.html; and http://cgis.jpost.com/Blogs/india/entry/the_bnei_menashe_could_benefit

[23] http://www.economist.com/world/asia/displaystory.cfm?story_id=12941078

[24] See: http://en.wikipedia.org/wiki/Lemba

[25] See: http://groups.yahoo.com/group/Sabbath_in_Africa/ ?yquid=72503

[26] See: http://www.bechollashon.org

[27] See Isaiah 49:19-23 and 54:2-3.

[28] Genesis 15:12. There are three additional references for these same boundaries: 1 Ki. 4:21; 2 Chr. 9:21; and Ps. 72:8. In ten other references, the covenants of the LORD are declared permanent and non-negotiable. It is ironic that both Yasser Arafat and Saddam Hussein were paranoid about these texts in the Hebrew Scriptures while large percentages of both Jews and Christians neither believe in their accuracy nor even know they exist!

[29] Revelation 7:9-10

[30] Revelation 21:2-3

[31] Jeremiah 31:35-36

EPILOGUE

So where do we go from here? Actually we've already considered the options, but lest you have passed over them far too quickly—or will soon forget them in this white-water affair which I'd like to label as the final sprint to the finish line, let's look back in these closing moments—

Midway in the section of *Looking at Ourselves* in Chapter 8 we should recall:

> *So just taking a good look at ourselves instead of chafing at where the barbarians are heading is what is now left of what we may yet be able to fix.*

> *Therefore, let us take a good look at ourselves as Westerners, where we as a body—as well as individually—have had our blind spots about how we really appear in the eyes of the Most High, and what we might yet do to turn our performance around a bit before His Messiah returns.*

And at the very end of that same section the ultimate corner that we must turn:

> *So as we take personal inventory, the Western worldview has prompted us to do some wonderful works, but perhaps the King of the Universe would be even more pleased if we garnished all of this with a bit more intimacy with Him!*

And also the wakeup call in the closing lines of Chapter 6:

> *This is not exactly a good time to say, "Amen." It's a good time to wake up and start saying sorry to the real God!*

Then last of all, our finale of encouragement as we close out Chapter 9:

> *"I have told you these things, so that in me you may have peace. In this world you will have trouble. But take heart! I have overcome the world."*

So keep that difference handy. The Ancient of Days will never tread on those end-of-days clay toes of His beloved!

FOR INTERNATIONAL MINISTRY SCHEDULE,
REQUESTS FOR MEETINGS, OR BOOKS CONTACT:

South Pacific Island Ministries, Inc.
PO Box 990, Smithfield 4878, Qld. Australia
Fax: (07) 4058-0258; International: (617) 4058-0258
E-mail: SpimAust@aol.com or info@spim.org.au
Visit our website at: http://www.spim.org.au

BOOK SALES IN USA:
Order from www.Amazon.com
Or available through any Christian bookstore.
Bulk sales for churches or non-profit organizations
(10 or more copies):
Bernhard Laubli, SPIM USA Rep. Email: spimusa@gmail.com

BOOK SALES IN AUSTRALIA:
CLC Bookworld, Koorong, Word or other Christian Bookshops.
For further information contact: SpimAust@aol.com
Also available at ICEJ Australia: icejaus@bigpond.com
Bridges for Peace at: adminaust@bridgesforpeace.com.au

BOOK SALES IN ISRAEL:
The Galilee Experience
PO Box 1693, Tiberias 14115
Tel: 04-672-3260 Toll free from USA: 1888 838-7928
E-mail: info@TheGalileeExperience.com

Emmanuel Bookshop
PO Box 14037, Jaffa Gate, Jerusalem 911140
Tel: 02-6277746 Fax: 02-626-3855
E-mail: emb_shop@netvision.net.il

(Book Sales in Israel continued on next page)

144

Kibbutz Ginosar Bookshop—Galilee
Tel: 04-671-2073 Email: mail@jesusboat.com

Greetings from Jerusalem—Vision for Israel
Email: info@visionforisrael.com Tel: 054-530-7075

International Christian Embassy Jerusalem
Email: resources@icej.org Tel: 02-539-9700

Christian Friends of Israel—Jerusalem
Email: CFI@cfijerusalem.org Tel: 02-623-3778

**FOR BOOK SALES IN THE UK, IRELAND, SOUTH AFRICA
OR OTHER INTERNATIONAL REQUESTS,**
contact SPIM, Inc. at SpimAust@aol.com
or www.Amazon.com

OTHER BOOKS BY VICTOR SCHLATTER:

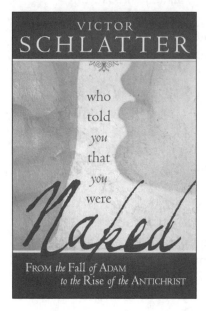

Who Told You that You Were Naked?

From the fall of Adam to the rise of the Antichrist, God is still asking same question. Rigor mortis has set into today's organized religion and there seems to be little understanding of the ramifications!

Although Adam and Eve ran quickly to hide themselves when they realized they were naked, the Church remains exposed to evil that replaces commitment to the Creator.

Victor Schlatter is a nuclear scientist turned linguist, turned church planter and prolific writer. His passion and clarity on the issues at hand are strikingly refreshing and stand out as solutions that work.

In *Who Told You that You Were Naked?* the author uncovers the naked truth about the issues in which the church should be fully engaged. He hangs his "Ninety-Five Theses" on the hearts of all those who love Him and His appearing. You will gain new understanding and be challenged to action concerning:

From the Garden of Eden to ancient Greece and Jerusalem, past 9-11 America to our post-modern world, Victor presents a biblically sound look at the serpent's continued deception:

Destiny Image Publishers, Shippensburg PA: 1-800-722-6774 or www.destinyimage.com

Where Is the Body?

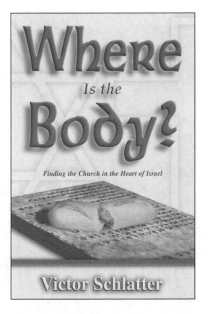

Where Is the Body? is different. With the author's over 40 years of experience in the Third World, it was inspired and written with insights far more compatible with an original Middle Eastern setting and far less jaded with twentieth century trends and assumptions.

It is our wake-up call in these unpredictable days of Israel's preparation and testing. Its purpose is to jar the church into an awakening of what the God of Abraham is methodically setting up in Israel as groundwork for the return of His Son. It challenges not a few threadbare end-time assumptions such as have been given a ride on the coat tails of anti-Semitic thought latent in many segments of the Church. Its aim is to provoke honest thought, and above all, faithfully cites the Bible you say you believe. It has been translated also into Russian, Finnish, and Dutch.

Where Is the Body? is an internationally endorsed release:

This is a fascinating and provocative book. Victor Schlatter exposes the anti-Semitism that so often distorts evangelical life and thought. He makes a strong case for a theology that centers on God's deep and abiding love for Israel and the Jewish people. I came away from reading his discussion with new insights of the biblical message.
—*Dr. Richard Mouw, PhD. President Fuller Theological Seminary, Pasadena, CA, USA.*

Destiny Image Publishers, Shippensburg PA: 1-800-722-6774 or www.destinyimage.com

Showdown of the Gods

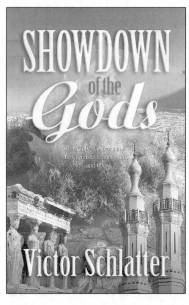

Ironically went to press on September 11, 2001. Today they play footsie together; tomorrow they kill each other. The sub-title says it best: *The Evening News Won't Surprise Old Zechariah.*

Showdown of the Gods connects the ancient biblical prophets to our morally and spiritually unravelling globe. It refocuses on commonplace disasters around us in the light of prophecy, while exposing the agenda of unlikely bedfellows—Islam and New World Order humanism—each vying for their own last day challenge to a Creator God. When expedient they feign friendship; when opportune they draw blood. Indeed, the evening news won't surprise old Zechariah!

Evergreen Press, Theodore AL: 1-888-670-7463,
info@evergreenpress.com

About the Author

Victor Schlatter spent seven years as a nuclear scientist before hearing a call from Above to upgrade his career to linguistics and Bible translation. In a South Pacific Stone Age scenario, he translated the *Waola* Scriptures, now in their 6th printing. He found that there is no such thing as a "primitive" language, since Stone Age *Waola* has over 100 endings on every verb. His translation has since spawned over 120 tribal congregations exceeding 10,000 believers across Papua New Guinea.

The Schlatters then reached out in a Pacific-wide ministry, tying Isaiah's oft repeated *"Islands of the Sea"* to the long-foretold Israel reborn. Having made annual trips to Jerusalem since 1988, he has kept up in-depth research of the broiling Middle East countdown, especially as it reflects biblical prophecy. He is Director of South Pacific Island Ministries, represents the International Christian Embassy Jerusalem to the South Pacific Islands, and lectures worldwide.

He was awarded the Queen's Papua New Guinea Independence Medal in 1975 for recognised service to the Southern Highlands, and was selected for Who's Who in Queensland, Australia in 2007. He is the author of *Where Is the Body?* (translated into Russian, Finnish and Dutch), *Showdown of the Gods*, and *Who Told You that You Were Naked?*

Victor and his wife, Elsie, currently live in Australia.

More on South Pacific Island Ministries is found on:
http://www.spim.org.au

1 Aug 2010
Dear Karen
Be Blessed in Yeshua